M~~aking~~

Learning

Communities

Work

The Critical Role
of Leader
as Learner

REBECCA VAN DER BOGERT
Winnetka Public Schools, Evanston, Illinois
Harvard Graduate School of Education

VOLUME EDITOR AND EDITOR-IN-CHIEF

MAKING LEARNING COMMUNITIES WORK: THE CRITICAL ROLE OF
LEADER AS LEARNER
Rebecca van der Bogert (ed.)
New Directions for School Leadership, No. 7, Spring 1998
Rebecca van der Bogert, Editor-in-Chief

© 1998 by Jossey-Bass Inc., Publishers.

Microfilm copies of issues and articles are available in 16mm and 35mm, as well as
microfiche in 105mm, through University Microfilms Inc., 300 North Zeeb Road,
Ann Arbor, Michigan 48106-1346.

ISSN 1089-5612   ISBN 0-7879-4272-3

NEW DIRECTIONS FOR SCHOOL LEADERSHIP is part of The Jossey-Bass Education
Series and is published quarterly by Jossey-Bass Inc., Publishers, 350 Sansome Street,
San Francisco, California 94104-1342.

SUBSCRIPTIONS: Please see Ordering Information on p. iv.
EDITORIAL CORRESPONDENCE should be sent to Rebecca van der Bogert, Winnetka
Public Schools, 2759 Eastwood Avenue, Evanston, Illinois 60201.

Jossey-Bass Web address: www.josseybass.com

Printed in the United States of America on acid-free recycled paper containing 100
percent recovered waste paper, of which at least 20 percent is postconsumer waste.

The International Network of Principals' Centers

The International Network of Principals' Centers sponsors *New Directions for School Leadership* as part of its commitment to strengthening leadership at the individual school level through professional development for leaders. The Network has a membership of principals' centers, academics, and practitioners in the United States and overseas and is open to all groups and institutions committed to the growth of school leaders and the improvement of schools. The Network currently functions primarily as an information exchange and support system for member centers in their efforts to work directly with school leaders in their communities. Its office is in the Principals' Center at the Harvard Graduate School of Education.

The Network offers these services:

- The International Directory of Principals' Centers features member centers with contact persons, descriptions of center activities, program references, and evaluation instruments.
- The Annual Conversation takes place every spring, when members meet for seminars, workshops, speakers, and to initiate discussions that will continue throughout the year.
- *Newsnotes*, the Network's quarterly newsletter, informs members of programs, conferences, workshops, and special interest items.
- *Reflections*, an annual journal, includes articles by principals, staff developers, university educators, and principals' center staff members.

For further information, please contact:

International Network of Principals' Centers
Harvard Graduate School of Education
336 Gutman Library
Cambridge, MA 02138
(617) 495-9812

Ordering Information

NEW DIRECTIONS FOR SCHOOL LEADERSHIP
This series of paperback books provides principals, superintendents, teachers, and others who exercise leadership at the local level with insight and guidance on the important issues influencing schools and school leadership. Books in the series are published quarterly in Spring, Summer, Fall, and Winter and are available for purchase both by subscription and individually.

SUBSCRIPTIONS cost $52.00 for individuals (a savings of 35 percent over single-copy prices) and $105 for libraries. Prices subject to change. There are no shipping and handling charges on subscriptions.

SINGLE COPIES cost $25.00 plus shipping. There will be handling charges on billed orders. Call the 800 number below for more information.

SINGLE COPIES AVAILABLE FOR SALE

QUANTITY DISCOUNTS ARE AVAILABLE. Please contact Jossey-Bass Periodicals for information at 1-415-433-1740.

TO ORDER, CALL 1-800-956-7739 or 1-415-433-1767
. . . and visit our website at www.josseybass.com

Contents

The International Network of Principals' Centers at the Harvard Graduate School of Education is a loosely coupled group of individuals who have interacted over the years around the challenge of providing environments in which leaders' growth flourishes. Our story is one of common searching, incessant questioning, and sharing of life's turns. One of the unplanned outcomes of our work has been the creation of a community of learners that supports our own growth. We'd like to bring you into our ever-expanding community. Let's begin with a description of a few of the characters, the setting, the plot, and the purpose of the community.

1

The story

Roland S. Barth, Rebacca van der Bogert

THIS IS a story, a story of over a decade of struggles and joys that we have shared. It is an unfolding journey, as we have come to love and understand one another's strengths and weaknesses and developed an implicit understanding of how to give and receive support from one another. We are a community of learners.

The story is a tapestry woven by many hands. It began at the Harvard Principals' Center and now has many ties throughout the world. The warp that binds it all together is a strong set of beliefs about teaching and learning. The color in the tapestry, as well as the driving force for continual weaving, is the ongoing quest to create environments in which adult growth flourishes.

Each of us involved in this tapestry confesses to either rebelling against our own learning experiences early in life or else such complete submission that it narrowed our soul until we got out from

NEW DIRECTIONS FOR SCHOOL LEADERSHIP, NO. 7, SPRING 1998 © JOSSEY-BASS PUBLISHERS

under traditional learning. Thus the common quest for ways in which learning can honor the individual's head, heart, and soul.

The characters

Let us begin by introducing what we've come to cherish about each of the characters in our story.

Richard the conversationalist

The author of our first chapter is Richard. When any of us wants to have a conversation that doesn't necessarily have to go anywhere but contributes to our thinking six months later, we call Richard. He brings to us a sense of leisure and being totally there for us at that moment. Richard Ackerman appropriately frames our journey through this sourcebook with the notion of conversation as a vehicle for learning. We've come to cherish the power of conversation and have discovered many reasons to engage in it. Several assumptions behind our work have bonded us together and brought us to the use of conversation in our quest to provide environments in which leaders can flourish:

- Principals hold within them an extraordinary amount of craft knowledge.
- Principals are astute in taking charge of their own learning and determining what it is they need to know and how they learn best.
- Principals have different needs, and their learning should be individualized.
- Sharing craft knowledge through conversation is a powerful means of growth that encompasses all of these assumptions.

Thus we hold an Annual Conversation in which participants from around the world hear little lecturing but engage in a great deal of structured and unstructured conversation about practice. We have learned, however, that conversation is a whole art form, one that needs to be practiced, nurtured, and challenged. In our quest for understanding the art form, we ourselves have engaged in our own learning from and about conversations.

Richard begins in the first chapter by capturing one of our many conversations on a set of rocks overlooking the Atlantic Ocean, as we conceptualized this journal. Hopefully, he shares some of his thinking about conversation also.

Gordy the anchor

Gordy's solid six-foot-three structure belies his personality. Gordy Donaldson is our anchor, at times keeping us balanced and reminding us that we need to produce in order to have our voices make a difference in the conversation. At other times he becomes mischievous and encourages those who are challenging us to bring things to the table. Gordy provides a safety net, while he makes us sweat. He also looks silly at times as he brings out his pom-poms to cheer us on to finish a piece of writing or face an angry school board member. Gordy's chapter is about his work with principals in the Maine Network of School Leaders as they work closely with one another exploring who they are as people and how they might find balance in their lives. In his chapter, you have an opportunity to listen in on a conversation of a small and collegial coaching group as they learn from their ongoing daily experiences as leaders in schools.

Vivian the reminder of diversity

Vivian Williams is our severely and intellectually forthright professor from Oxford, who loyally joins us and reminds us how homogeneous we are and how odd some of our practices look from the eyes of someone from outside the United States. He does this, of course, with his well-developed sense of astringent humor.

One of our strong beliefs from the inception of our Network has been the richness that we gain from diversity. We have found that some of our greatest development is when we are challenged by someone coming from a totally different perspective and bringing a new set of eyes. Among the most vivid examples of this are the interactions that have taken place among leaders from different countries. When one is confronted with a question such as, "How are leadership issues of African principals who walk twenty miles to school every morning similar to mine?" one can't help but broaden one's thinking. This is the kind of conversation that takes place at the Norham Leadership Centre at Oxford as Vivian gathers principals from around the world to discuss their development as leaders. Vivian shares some of his experiences with us in his chapter.

Gayle the mom

At the risk of sounding sexist, Gayle is our eternal mom. She's always quietly in the background, seeing that things are brought together; although deflecting the spotlight, she gains great satisfaction from others' accomplishments. If she can't be there, her presence is felt in her planning, the wise words that come from those she sends to our meetings, and her model of sharing credit with everyone. Gayle has worked with the Florida Leadership Center for many years and in her chapter shares some specific activities that encompass the elements we find underlying successful experiences to nurture growth. You will see what we mean by *mom*.

David the spirit

Dave Hagstrom is our spiritual leader, the one who always brings us back to the quiet peace within ourselves. With his permission, we share a letter he sent two days after the closing of our Third Annual Conversation:

I awoke early this morning feeling blessed and deeply touched by the events of the past three days. I feel that your words to us on that final day captured the essence of the spiritual bridge that is connecting so many of us and compelling us to return to Conversation after Conversation. For many of us, this Network is becoming a significant professional home and the Annual Conversation is becoming a time of genuine, even powerful, professional renewal.

Imagine the new insight that was mine as I heard others at the Conversation expressing feelings similar to mine following your remarks to the group. It was then that I began to truly feel that spiritual connection that is this Network and to really appreciate the understanding that you have about the nature of this process of which we are a part. We are each caught up in a pioneering effort, aren't we? And it's this new awareness of the nature of the effort that I consider the special gift that's been given to me these past few days. These are gifted men and women we work with, and there's a quality of "genius" present within each one that is celebrated quite beautifully in one another's presence. I guess we've created our own safe harbor where it's OK to "not know," and because it's safe ground, we go on to quietly recommit ourselves, those fine and special visions we hold for children, our school, and ourselves.

David shares some of the activities that bring this same sense of spirituality and safe harbor into the leadership academies he has led.

Joe and the power of struggles

The chapter after David's is filled with the most visible struggles. Naturally, this is written by Joe Richardson, who constantly reminds us how much we cherish the opportunity to share our shortcomings with one another. Joe demonstrates this well, partly through modeling his own humility and being able to poke fun at himself and partly by sharing so visibly the struggles that all of us have had. In his words, "We all learn best from our warts." Joe has been one of our bravest souls; he gave up his job at the university level and took on the leadership of a school to see if he could bring to life some of his thinking about the growth of adults. Although from most people's perspective Joe was successful at nurturing a community of learners in his own school, he shares his thoughts about the ongoing complexities of such a task, the obstacles and realities of trying to make it happen, and the fact that he is left with more questions now than when he began.

Becky the idealist

Becky is our incurable idealist, constantly conflicted between the need to be part of a group that enhances her own learning, similar to the Network, and the need to get involved in places that aren't that way to see if they can be made so. She can't resist living out "If not us, who?" and "If not now, when?" Becky shares her attempts at contributing to an environment in public school settings that honors some of the values from the Network that she has come to hold so dear.

Roland the anarchist

Then there's Roland. Roland Barth. He would deflect the use of the word *leader* in regard to his role in the Network, but I think he is comfortable with the fact that certain of his personal qualities serve as part of the magnetic force that keeps us together. Roland's ability to articulate what we've all been mulling around intuitively helps us clarify what we're doing. His visionary spirit, playfulness with ideas, love of metaphors, and flirtatious anarchy serve as real cornerstones for many of our discussions. His constant search into the future and wondering about leadership is evident as he looks back to his own schooling at Puddle Dock and ahead to schools of the twenty-first century.

The setting

Recently one of our colleagues, Phil Hallinger, sent us a story from Thailand that he heard about a local villager. It serves as a wonderful metaphor for the journey we're about to describe. It goes like this.

A villager in northeast Thailand volunteered weekly at the Buddhist temple, cleaning up the grounds. They had him picking grass and weeds out of the ground to make it look clean. One day he noticed that the insects lived in the grass and thought about how people live beneath the trees. That inspired him to realize how few trees were left on the grounds.

He had the idea of planting tree saplings on the grounds of the temple; he consulted the abbot. The abbot was skeptical but went along with it as long as it wasn't going to cost anything. Well, the man started collecting saplings from the edge of the woods on the land that he farmed and planting them in the temple. People said he was crazy when he told them of his idea of having the shade of trees throughout the temple (the temple grounds were quite large). They said, "You'll be dead by the time any trees you plant now really grow into something."

He went at it one tree at a time, year in and year out. Some trees died, but he learned as he went along which trees liked which types of soil and came to know how to grow the trees. It was his faith in the importance of what he was doing that allowed him to carry on through the years as people laughed, as trees died, and during the many times when he worked alone.

Gradually he ran out of trees to plant from his own land and had to ask for help from his neighbors and friends. They saw that the trees were really growing into beautiful wooded grounds. So they helped him by contributing small saplings from their own land, though many still shook their heads at his efforts. In fact, after a number of years, not only had he started running out of small trees but also he ran out of room to plant trees in the temple grounds. So he began to plant trees elsewhere in the village.

Fourteen years later the temple now has beautiful shaded grounds. The village's square and parks are filled with shade trees, which provide a home for the local people. The vision of the now-old man has come into being, one tree at a time, nurtured by his faith, persistence, and learning.

This story holds particular poignancy in Thailand, where the forests are being destroyed daily. Moreover, the government has engaged in a largely vain attempt at reforestation—vain attempt because the people who plant the trees are simply told to do it. They have quotas, but no faith. Lacking faith, they don't take the time to learn nor give the care needed to nurture life.

The Harvard Principals' Center may have first gotten the idea to plant trees in the form of a Principal Center, and it may have even planted the first tree. But now the world is forested with trees planted by hundreds of other heroic, educational "villagers" around the globe. Each has struggled with issues of soil, faith, persistence, and learning.

Harvard University has enormous virtues. It also has its peculiarities. Being considered by many to be one of the world's greatest academic institutions—and our country's most venerable one—has both advantages and disadvantages for those within the university and without.

One distinct advantage *and* disadvantage is that any activity, no matter how inconsequential, conducted under the imprimatur of

Harvard is quickly noted by those outside the university. Thus, a new activity is not only noted but is seen as noteworthy. We used to call this the "burden of presumed competency."

Thus it was not surprising that within weeks of launching the Principals' Center at Harvard in the fall of 1980, the word was out that "they have started a principals' center at Harvard." It was not totally clear to those of us running the center just what a principals' center was or even whether the idea had merit.

Soon, phone calls—and visitors—began to stream in from other universities, from state departments of education, from school districts, even from foreign countries. What *is* a principals' center? Why is Harvard doing this? How did you get it going? How do you fund a center? How is the program for principals determined? The interest and the energy of others soon rivaled our own. One of us was asked to address these and other questions at the annual conference of the National Staff Development Council.

The precarious resources of our fledgling center were being depleted not only from within by some five hundred Boston-area principals but also from without. We could have consumed all of our resources just keeping our attention on our knitting. Instead, late one afternoon, on the third floor of Gutman Library, we decided rather spontaneously to create a national network of principals' centers. More accurately, we decided to acknowledge, reify, and tend the informal, vigorous network that was already fast-developing. In a word, we decided to institutionalize what already was.

Although it was a spur-of-the-moment decision, several important considerations supported it. Foremost among them was the realization that the Harvard Center and the International Network of Principals' Centers were and still are inseparable. In the big picture, a principals' center is about acknowledging, sharing, and celebrating within the community of school principals the abundant craft that exists out there about school leadership. Who is to say which principals in which systems in which states or countries are to be included? Clearly, we thought, the more the better. The concept of community has no boundaries.

Secondly, Harvard being Harvard, the inquiries and the parade of visitors were going to continue, whether welcomed or not. "Build it and they will come," indeed! Energies would be expended one way or another. How much better to spend our efforts welcoming rather than rejecting those intrigued by the idea of a principals' center.

Linking the Harvard Principals' Center with the International Network of Principals' Centers works both ways. Fledgling, struggling, new centers in Atlanta, St. Louis, or New Orleans all desperately need resources and recognition, but they desperately need something else in order to get them: legitimacy. The novel nature of the concept of a principals' center renders it, in the arcane world of schools and universities, subject to appearing "flaky," lacking both "rigor" and "respectability." ("What? Attendance by principals is *voluntary?*" "You mean *principals* decide what they need to know and be better able to do?" "What does a day at a ropes course have to do with school reform?")

So the close affiliation with the National Network of Principals' Centers at Harvard offered the fledgling centers as much as it offered the Harvard Principals' Center. As one principals' center leader observed, "We can all make good use of that 'burden of presumed competence'!" A win-win.

Put differently, what should be (but isn't) respectable without the Harvard name tag may become respectable with it. Perhaps bestowing legitimacy on vulnerable yet promising new ideas is the greatest contribution reputable universities can make to improve our society.

Thus was born an enduring, reciprocal relationship between the Harvard Principals' Center and what is now the International Network of Principals' Centers at Harvard, encompassing scores of other individual centers around the globe.

A few years later, the Network had become such a vigorous "growth industry" that Roland Barth's position changed from director of the Harvard Principals' Center to codirector in charge of outreach, that is, the Network. Ken Haskins in turn became the codirector of the Harvard Principals' Center in charge of its activities with Boston-area principals. The two functions were split.

Yet many activities continue to bridge the two, such as the annual ten-day summer institute run by the Harvard Principals' Center for school leaders from around the world, many of whom attend intent upon starting centers of their own back home.

The plot

While all of these centers were springing up around the country and the world, we struggled with the productive tension of a commitment to diversity and a need to define a clear mission to bond us together. Through many conversations, we began to clarify these unifying beliefs.

The beliefs about teaching and learning are both commonsense and commonplace in school literature. We see they are indeed universal across the human experience, if we examine the literature from early childhood education to adult development. They have stood the test of time, as is obvious if you read the literature from Socrates to Dewey to Gardner.

The reality, however, is that embodying these beliefs in learning experiences is rare. What the individuals in this community of learners have learned is that creating environments encompassing these beliefs requires greater effort on the part of individuals, evokes issues of accountability from many, and is hard to assess in terms of quantitative results. Though we are filled with success stories from principals and teachers, and we instinctively know when an activity works, we are still confronted by those who want to see direct correlation to raised test scores and more rigor and book learning.

Over the years, we've spent fruitful hours discussing our various beliefs about teaching and learning. Of course, there are many such beliefs, and we don't all hold exactly the same ones. But at the core of most of our conversations, we find a commitment to these beliefs:

- People learn best when they are invested in and make significant decisions about their own learning.

- People learn best when they are learning something of immediate interest and use to them.
- People learn best through real-life experiences.
- People learn at different rates and in different ways.
- People have a need to learn and grow that emerges given the right conditions.

Though these beliefs have stood the test of time for us, we find them markedly absent from the current dialogue about education in our country. Instead we hear mandates from all directions, emerging from certain assumptions:

- A hierarchy must exist within learning organizations in order for them to run efficiently.
- Those at the top of the hierarchy know what needs to be known by everyone in the organization.
- Those at the top of the hierarchy are responsible for evaluating everyone and delineating what each person's deficits are.
- These deficits represent what the individual is mandated to learn in order for the organization to run most efficiently.

The purpose

In the following chapters, we hope to share our community with others. We'd like to bring you into our conversations and share some of our struggles as well as our successes. This is an opportunity for us to try to make sense of what we've learned over the years and clarify the questions that emerge as we unpeel the layers of what we're learning.

We are not offering this as a prototype of a community of learners. Each community takes its own shape. Some elements can perhaps be extrapolated, but as we all know each community is different by virtue of who the individuals are within the community. How we function as a community, the common quests that we take on, and how we gather together *works for us*. We want to share this with you. We do this not out of smugness that we have any answers about communities of learners, but out of a need to share one of the most precious experiences of life.

ROLAND S. BARTH *is a former public school teacher and principal and founding director of the Harvard Principals' Center and senior lecturer on education at the Harvard Graduate School of Education. He writes and sails in Florida and Maine.*

REBECCA (BECKY) VAN DER BOGERT *is superintendent of schools in Winnetka, Illinois, and codirector of the International Network of Principals' Centers at the Harvard Graduate School of Education.*

Connecting in a special way through conversation is at the heart of our gatherings. At first, those moments seemed to be a natural happening and were taken for granted. With time, however, we realized we had a great deal to learn about the art of conversation. Thus we've made a conscious effort to reflect on our conversations and how they contribute to our learning. All of this is done while holding on to the magic and naturalness that we all cherish. Richard reflects on one of our favorite approaches to the art of conversation and what it yields for common understanding.

2

A conversation on the rocks

Richard H. Ackerman

I must go down to the seas again, for the call of the running tide
Is a wild call and a clear call that may not be denied;
And all I ask is a windy day with the white clouds flying,
And the flung spray and the blown spume, and the sea-gulls crying.
John Masefield, "Sea-Fever"

THE CONVERSATION I'm about to relay started on the smooth granite rocks that form the New England shoreline in front of my home overlooking the Atlantic Ocean. A number of us who have been associated with the Network for some time—Becky van der Bogert, Bob Wimpelberg, Sue Rubel, Gordy Donaldson, Joe Richardson, Roland Barth, Linda Holloman, and Vivian Williams—ambled down the crooked path to those old rocks on a nippy New England morning to engage in what we like to think of as a conversation.

NEW DIRECTIONS FOR SCHOOL LEADERSHIP, NO. 7, SPRING 1998 © JOSSEY-BASS PUBLISHERS

Our purpose was to discuss what this journal might be about and how it would come together. It was a perfect New England day: windy with white clouds flying and seagulls crying, as the poem says. The faint hum of a foghorn from Gloucester light could be heard in the distance.

Geologically speaking, only a short time has elapsed since the glacial retreat that formed this magnificent New England coast. Each of us spent a few more minutes finding our "place" on these old water-tumbled granite boulders and sheets in preparation for our conversation. It's remarkable to remember that this granite was once molten material, heated and then cooled into a rock crust, slowly worn down by water, wind, freezing, and thawing, sun, rain, and perhaps even the prying roots of plants like the ornery poison ivy that has managed miraculously to thrive here and surround us now. The size of these different granite crystals—quartz, feldspar, and hornblende—is determined by the time they needed to collect while the rock was cooling and solidifying. Each with its own colors, surface texture, and cleavage patterns is now fused for another seeming eternity.

It was a humbling thought at the start of this conversation—perhaps, of any conversation—to consider the miracle of how these extraordinary rocks were formed, of how they got here at all, and indeed of how and why ideas ever get anywhere at all. Sitting together on those old rocks, with nothing but a clear blue horizon in front of us so that our eyes didn't have to focus narrowly, the way they usually do in front of our printed words and computer screens, we were reminded how much we, as old friends, had become kindred spirits too. Like these old, beautiful, rocky crystalline structures, we too are a fused community; we come together in the interest of cultivating ways for school leaders to improve their leadership so as to benefit the children of their schools. The International Network of Principals' Centers is simply that: a means for ideas, practices, and learning about school leadership development to be shared as widely as possible. Ours is a community of learning; it is richest when it honors all learners, celebrates their questions, supports their quest for insight, and nurtures these insights into actions that help leaders grow. Most important, our community has thrived through conversation: sharing experiences among people living with the maxim that all members bring value to the circle.

Our conversation that morning had an ebb and flow just like the waves breaking on the rocks below, ideas coming and going and changing with a rhythm that is as salty and unpredictable as the sea. The surface of the ocean is rarely quiet. Even when the wind isn't blowing and collecting water into waves, the open water is moving up and down. Swells created by storms or weather patterns hundreds or thousands of miles away move majestically and inevitably onward until they reach a coast like this one. They pile up on the rocks and fall back, sometimes covering only a few inches, but often many feet. For this reason, it is difficult to talk about high tide and low tide as though each were a single precise level that the water reaches on an open shore. It's not that exact, and of course this is also what is wonderful about a conversation. You just can't be sure at what levels it rises or falls.

We talked, as we often do, in metaphors. One that immediately grabbed and engulfed us like a good wave, and then stuck like plankton, was the idea of "the two sets of books." Each of us interpreted this metaphor in our own way, but the general idea went something like this.

As we look at our work in schools, most of us encounter a number of well-intentioned constituencies—parents, teachers, students, administrative staff—each with its own important agendas and reasons for doing the things its members believe are important to do. If we look carefully at the various agendas of these groups (through a Venn diagram, for example), we probably see many places where the groups agree and many places where they don't. The weight of somehow keeping these various groups and agendas all heading in the same direction, while at the same time honoring the different kinds of things each group wants, usually filters to the school leader (or someone designated as such). How do well-intentioned school leaders find ways to integrate these various agendas—bringing two sets of books into one?

A majority of people who spend their lives in educational institutions, and who are aware at some level of at least two sets of books in their world, believe having two sets of books (at least) is the best way to do, be, and learn. Why must we operate under two sets of books? To what extent do we in schools engage in what are called trade-offs: bargains that trade off rules, values, and principles for the sake of keeping the peace? It seemed to us that the challenge in schools is not to bring people into dogmatically believed-in beliefs but rather to try to bring all these sets of books into sync with who we truly are as learners and as leaders. So our conversation on the rocks turned to the question, How do we keep *one* set of books? Specifically, how do we develop a kind of honesty and authenticity in language and form, structure, behavior, and relationship with one another that reflects one set of books?

Since its inception, the Network has relied upon and thrived on the art and craft of conversation as a means of articulating one set of books. However, the elements that form the basis for what we call a "conversation" suggest a process that is actually quite disorderly and messy. We fully recognize that our so-called understandings of conversation freeze in time what remains a mysterious and magnificent process for humans: talking with one another. Our purpose has never been to foster a pedagogical orthodoxy around this process. Rather, it is to affirm and celebrate a framework for looking at how people make sense of their experience and what they do with the sense they make. Our own explorations validate for us that conversation is something that people do naturally at a fundamental level of meaning making.

Conversation is a form of communication by which a group of people discover the shared meaning that moves among and through the group. *Shared meaning*, or meaning common to a group, is the basis of culture building and making. If one were to walk around a school or any organization and simply listen in on the conversations, one would develop a keen sense of the culture. In a conversation, one becomes aware of the underlying preconceived thoughts, feelings, and conclusions that come from belonging to a particular culture, or a similar culture. However, in any group of people, there are bound to be some with different assumptions and things they do not share. Still, disagreeing on one point needn't keep us from hearing other perspectives. The more we share, the quicker it might change the one point of disagreement. In everyday conversations, people usually express their points of view with the purpose of convincing or persuading others. Since individual points of view differ widely, group discussions and conversations can divide and polarize participants. There is a tendency to defend one's own opinions and adopt uncompromising positions.

A conversation that seeks one set of books potentially encourages participants to suspend attachment to a particular point of view (or opinion) so the group can achieve deeper levels of attention, synthesis, and feeling. In this kind of conversation, each person tries to discover a deeper meaning behind the opinions that are expressed, abandoning the desire to be right and see who is wrong. Individual differences are valued and respected. A broader and more expansive perspective for all the participants can then be reached, establishing a different kind of relationship. The group then tries to create a more complete picture of reality instead of separating it into fragments or parts; one does not try to convince others of one's own point of view. This can lead to a greater understanding on the part of the whole group.

Conversation thus can potentially inform and build without pursuing a defined result. A very simple and powerful technique, for example, is to leave a space after each person's contribution to the conversation. By leaving a noticeable space of silence between contributions, the rhythm of the conversation slows down, allowing time for listening and reflecting at deeper levels. The group moves from a level of competition and exclusion to one of collaboration, association, and participation. A good conversation has the capacity to create an environment that fosters trust and promotes communication through an attitude of respect. Diversity among people is valued as an essential element.

We live in a world of relationship where the individual affects the group and the group has an impact on the individual. Problems arise when we behave as if the opposite were true—as if we lived in a fragmented world where the individual parts are separate from each other. We need to develop a new way of thinking and talking so we can perceive a different way of seeing. We could achieve this by first noticing and examining how we think. On the one hand, we say we want to live in peace and harmony; on the other, our separate thinking, talking, and way of seeing do not always correspond with this intention. Our individual thought process is often limited and incomplete. The fact that we do not see it operating complicates recognizing the role it plays as a cause of many of our conflicts.

In a conversation, the whole structure of defensiveness, opinions, and division has the potential to change; suddenly, the feeling may change to one of participation and sharing. When we share only opinions, we get the feeling we are participating. But having an attitude of defensiveness, holding our assumptions, sticking to them, and saying "I've got to be right" can leave the conversation very limited, because good conversations often require that we *not* defend an assumption. The foundation of an assumption or an opinion is that it is open to evidence that it may *not* be right. This does not mean we should impose the opinions on the group. Everybody may (or may not) have different opinions; it is not that important. It isn't necessary that everyone be persuaded to have the same view. This sharing of mind—of consciousness—is more important than the content of the opinions. And we may see that these opinions are limited, anyway. We may find that the answer is not in the opinions at all, but somewhere else!

One set of books doesn't emerge from opinions; it usually emerges from something else—perhaps from mere movement of this tacit mind. So we have to work on making meaning coherent if we are to perceive or find one set of books. This is why conversation is useful. Underneath, all the rocks are the same because of the very fact they are rocks: they are rigid. The idea of conversation is that we all share our place on the rocks and see the meaning of all of them.

Conversation is a means to discover these tendencies. By offering our individual perspectives in an environment where judgments are not automatically expressed, we make it possible to glimpse a broader vision. We can begin to perceive the connections between our actions and their results. We can incorporate a relational and participatory way of thinking. We can expand our understanding by simply learning to ask questions that lead to new levels of understanding. Each participant in a conversation has the responsibility and opportunity to push the understandings and learnings of a group. One can become conscious of one's own and others' rational processes and of the points that separate or unite us. In this respect, conversation can lead us to a shared basic perception, to a greater sensitivity in perceiving subtle meanings around us, and perhaps to one set of books.

RICHARD H. ACKERMAN *is associate professor at the University of Massachusetts Lowell and a lecturer on education at the Harvard Graduate School of Education.*

*One of our ongoing challenges in the Network is to create
forums in which leaders are free to take risks and feel secure
enough to share their vulnerabilities. Colleagues in the
Maine Network of School Leaders have created support-and-
development teams of three to five fellow leader-learners who
meet regularly in such forums. This is a conversation from
one of their meetings.*

3

Sharing the challenges: Critic-colleague teams and leadership development

Gordon A. Donaldson Jr.

THE FOUR of us are seated at student desks pulled together into a rectangle. Coffee mugs, potato chips, papers, and pens cover our space. Peter, Sarah, and I all lean forward on our elbows, intent on Sharon's words. It's late afternoon and we're at Peter's school for the monthly meeting of our support-and-development, or S&D, team. Peter is an elementary school principal, Sarah a middle school teacher leader, Sharon a high school principal, and I'm the coordinator of our leadership network. All Maine Network members belong to an S&D team, a small colleague-critic group that serves as the "base camp" for our leadership growth activities.

Now, an hour into our session, it's Sharon's turn to consult with us about what's currently challenging her in her work as principal.

"My intrapersonal challenge is about being judgmental," she says, relating what she understands of her internal self in leadership

NEW DIRECTIONS FOR SCHOOL LEADERSHIP, NO. 7, SPRING 1998 © JOSSEY-BASS PUBLISHERS

situations. I know this about myself: one of the reasons I stop listening to people in meetings is that I've decided they're uninformed, misguided, flat-out wrong. I'm sitting in a meeting, trying to get people to at least agree on some common points, and someone gets on a soapbox and blabbers. Inside my head, I'm saying, 'Right! Sure! What the hell does he know about what he's talking about?' Then I begin planning what I'll say next . . . before he's even finished."

"God, Sharon, I do the same thing!" Peter adds. "But what exactly is it that makes you turn off like this? What do you mean, 'judgmental'?"

Sharon ponders for a few seconds. "It's really very simple. Some people just don't know what they're talking about. They're uninformed about the kids we discuss. They haven't prepared for the meeting. They're more interested in covering their butts than coming up with a solution that works for kids. As soon as I see this, my mind just shuts down on them. They're wasting my time and probably everybody else's."

Sarah joins in with a question for Sharon. "So, you've identified this as your intrapersonal challenge. Why do you want to change this part of your leadership?"

"I guess from our discussions and reading I've seen how this type of behavior cuts me off from people I'm trying to lead. I mean, how can you be collaborative if you're not giving some of your collaborators the time of day?"

Peter jumps back in. "Yeah, I know what you mean. I think I do the same thing sometimes. With some people on my faculty, I've gotten to the point where I prejudge them. I don't expect to get anything of quality from them even before they come to a committee meeting! That's not good."

"As a teacher, I know exactly what you mean," Sarah adds. "The last principal at my school used to do that a lot. It got so some of us stopped even trying to take part in some conversations."

Turning eagerly to Sharon, Peter asks, "So, Sharon, have you thought about what you can do about this? I mean, I face the same thing and can learn a thing or two here!"

"Well, what I've written on my LDP [leadership development

plan] is that I've got to work on patience and tolerance. I'm going to start by trying to ring a little bell in my head when I'm being judgmental and starting to shut off to someone. I dunno. Something like . . . count to twenty in my head before saying anything to someone, or talking after someone who I'm convinced is wrong."

"So, you're going to try to stay interpersonally open to these people?" I ask, referring to how she interacts with staff.

"I'm not sure what you mean."

"I guess what I mean is that you seem to be focusing on controlling your gut reaction to what some people say so that you don't convey to them that you disagree or, worse, devalue them. There seem to be two parts to this: first, making yourself aware that you're feeling judgmental; second, changing how you usually act toward them interpersonally."

"I hadn't thought it through that way yet, but I suppose that's what I'm feeling. Right now, I just know that my judging isn't good for me or for the meetings I'm trying to run. What happens is that I get all worked up in the meeting and then afterwards I find myself having arguments with the person in my mind. I mean, I come out of a night meeting and rant and rave all the way home in the car, or to Dave when I get home."

"Oh, doesn't that sound familiar!" Peter laughs. "You know, it's just impossible to avoid this if you care deeply about kids and the school. You go to a meeting and there's always somebody who's just so far off-base. It can send the meeting off on a birdwalk. Or if the person's influential, it can lead to plain dumb decisions!"

"That's what really riles me," Sharon says. "But I've learned that if I let my feelings show, I can make the meeting even worse. I mean, it doesn't help any for me to blurt out something like, 'How did you come up with that?' It just creates hard feelings. As leaders, we're supposed to be trying to build consensus."

Sarah asks again, "So, what do you think will help you in these situations? How will you meet this intrapersonal challenge?"

"Like I said, I'm going to work on patience and tolerance in meetings . . . I'm going to try to use that little warning bell." Sharon reviews the sheet of paper in front of her where she's sketched out her leadership development plan. "I'm just going to try to control my impulse to judge, not to start composing my answer to someone before they've finished speaking. I'm going to work on my listening skills."

We all think about this for several moments. Then I speak. "That sounds like a good strategy for helping to keep the meeting positive. It would be good to get more specific about exactly what listening behaviors you can use in these situations. I mean, if your alarm bell goes off, how will you act differently toward these people than you usually do?"

"Yeah," Sarah says. "I was wondering that too. With our old principal, we knew instantly when he was shutting down. I'll bet some of the people on your staff know that, too. How can your nonverbal cues tell them that you're actually hearing them?"

"I've been thinking about that, too," Sharon answers. "I haven't written anything out yet, but this is where my intrapersonal goal and my interpersonal goal meet. I've got to dig out those articles about active listening and see if there's something I can use. When the alarm bell rings, I've got to be able to show the person I think is wrong that I'm still open to his view."

We discuss Sharon's need for new listening strategies. Members of the group make suggestions and ask further clarifying questions. Sarah even remarks on Sharon's attentiveness to people in the S&D team, saying, "I have a hard time picturing you judging and shutting out at school." Sharon jots notes to herself on her LDP and concludes with a promise to "journal" about these ideas and try out one or two in meetings in the coming two weeks.

Then the conversation takes a new turn as Sarah asks, "But what are you going to do with your real feelings about these people? You seem to be stuffing them in a closet, and I don't know if that's good for you. . . ."

I add, "Yeah, I was wondering about that too. Your plans sound good for the committee and the school, but if you're convinced that someone is wrong and concerned that their wrongheadedness might lead to something bad for the school or for a child, should you be sitting on those feelings?"

Sharon thinks about this for a second. "I don't see that I have much of a choice. I've told you what happens sometimes when I speak out. I think I've got to keep on stuffing it."

Then Peter weighs in. "I don't know if it's an either-or. Have you thought about ways to express your disagreement with someone that might not shut them down? Or ways to turn what they've said back to the group so they can evaluate it?"

"I'm just not very good at that, Peter. I know what all that stuff about collaboration says, but it takes too much time and patience."

"Yeah," I interject. "But, Sharon, if you just stuff your real feelings in a closet, it's going to eat away at you. You're still going to be ranting and raving on the way home from meetings or beating Dave over the head with things you wished you'd said to someone else."

"I know, I know. You guys are going to have to help me figure out ways to say these things. I can't live without speaking my mind. It's just that my usual old point-blank straight talk makes some people defensive."

Sharon's turn in her S&D team meeting is about to end. In her half-hour of consultation with Peter, Sarah, and me, she has grappled with a leadership challenge at the center of her work as a principal: can she remain interpersonally open to all her staff? The cost of not doing so is that she loses some of them; after all, who is going to follow a leader who doesn't give them the time of day? She's making progress understanding herself as she interacts with staff; we refer to this as her interpersonal knowledge.

With help from her S&D team, Sharon has discovered the link between this interpersonal challenge and her own internal workings, her judgmental thoughts about a staff member and her feelings about them as members of the faculty. This intrapersonal knowledge—her knowledge of her internal self in leadership situations—is linked in essential ways to her interpersonal behavior in meetings. Until she devises ways to handle her judgmental thoughts about a teacher's ideas and her sometimes disdainful feelings about the teacher, she's going to find it difficult to be interpersonally open and professionally respectful toward that teacher. She has made great strides by acknowledging how she is contributing to her own challenges as a leader.

In our Maine Network of School Leaders, Sharon's is the kind of exploration into leadership that we all strive for. It's frank, and it grapples with "a live one": a challenge that's interfering with her effectiveness and causing her to worry. S&D teams of three to five fellow leader-learners are the heart of our Network (you might even say they *are* the Network). Their supportiveness, probing, and questioning push and pull each of us to new understandings about the challenges we've identified as obstacles in our leadership effectiveness. Although we share readings and hear from outside experts on school leadership, these merely give us a wider selection of concepts, skills, and practices to choose from as we design our own ways to lead better.

We all have leadership development plans: written assessments and specific plans to operate differently (and hopefully better) as a leader in our own particular role and context. Sharon brought her LDP to her S&D team meeting. It represents her most recent thinking about what her challenges are and how she might address them. She begins her half-hour of consultation by bringing her team up to date on her actions, thoughts, and feelings. As her colleague-critics, we try—mostly through probing questions—to extend and deepen Sharon's thinking about what she might do to meet her challenges, both intrapersonal and interpersonal. Our goal is to have her leave our S&D team meeting with a refined plan for how she can act the next time the judgmental alarm bell rings in a meeting.

The evolution of her thinking follows an increasingly well-worn path in our Network. She moves from broad and vague plans to more specific, concrete, practical strategies. She moves from seeing the problem as residing mostly in others to understanding how it resides within herself as well. She moves from feeling frustrated with others to having some leads for how she might act in the future that will both ease those frustrations and facilitate meetings to be more inclusive.

Our Network is sustained by conversations like this because everybody present learns from the leadership experiences of everybody else. Peter, another principal, identifies immediately with Sharon's challenge. Sarah, a teacher leader, recognizes it in her former principal and perhaps in others who lead in her building. I connect with Sharon's dilemma because I've seen in many leaders— including myself—the unhealthy consequences of burying one's thoughts and feelings in the closet for the good of the school. Sharon's leadership development challenges teach us a lot about our own.

After a two-to-three-hour S&D team meeting and some large-group sharing with other teams, we all leave with more than we can process. But we also leave with notes on our LDPs as a place to begin thinking, feeling, and behaving in slightly altered ways, starting tomorrow. It's been another incremental step toward better leadership for us all. We look forward to the next Network gathering a month hence.[1]

Note

1. For more information about the model and practice of leadership development described here, see Donaldson, G. A., Jr., and Marnik, G. F. *Becoming Better Leaders.* Thousand Oaks, Calif.: Corwin Press, 1995.

GORDON A. DONALDSON JR. *is coordinator of the Maine Network of School Leaders and a professor at the University of Maine.*

Early in the history of our network of principals' centers, we discovered the power of conversations among leaders from different countries. We are now an International Network of Principals' Centers, with leaders from close to thirty countries sharing experiences similar to what you read about in this chapter.

4

International sharing as reflective images

Vivian Williams

FOLLOWING DEMANDS for educational reform during the late 1970s and 1980s, zealous Conservative governments mandated unprecedented changes in the education system of England and Wales. Reforms in school governance, management, curriculum, and student assessment were introduced. Policies predicated on concepts of "market forces" in education were intended to create a new client-focused system displacing earlier provider-led traditions (Williams, 1995). Through a series of education acts, especially the pivotal 1988 act, the structure and organization of schooling in England and Wales experienced fundamental reform, with teachers, students, parents, and communities traversing uncharted landscapes (Maclure, 1989).

The process of change invariably produces responses to meet challenges that demand new strategies and skills. The Norham Centre for Leadership Studies (NCLS) at the University of Oxford reflected one response to foreshadowed educational reform.

NEW DIRECTIONS FOR SCHOOL LEADERSHIP, NO. 7, SPRING 1998 © JOSSEY-BASS PUBLISHERS

Founded in 1987, its raison d'être arose from earlier exploratory studies about the changing requirements for leadership in education in response to new societal expectations. Government reforms provided both the opportunity and specific timing for creating NCLS as a focus for extended study and research in leadership. A major objective has been to facilitate sharing of experience and understanding of leadership behavior among educators at local, regional, and especially international levels. The international dimension is an important responsibility for NCLS. It has enabled the author to combine his extensive experience in providing training programs for education leaders in several local education authorities (LEAs) with appointments as visiting professor at various universities in the United States since the 1970s, following earlier positions as a school leader and LEA administrator.

In the United Kingdom, the legislative watershed initiated sweeping educational change during the early 1990s, for example, local management of schools (LMS, or site-based management), abolition of school zoning constraints, new freedoms for parental choice, a national curriculum throughout the statutory school years (ages five to sixteen), cyclical external school inspections, and teacher appraisal (evaluation).

Although organizationally complex, NCLS program goals were relatively clear from inception. As headteachers and principals are *the* pivotal persons in determining the quality of educational provision in schools, it is important to recognize that during implementation of organizational innovation the understanding, insights, and executive action of school leaders inevitably shape opportunities for their colleagues and students, for whom they are directly responsible.

These concerns were prioritized at the inaugural international NCLS conference at St. Peter's College in 1989. The top priority was identified as *Quis custodiet ipsos custodes* ("Who guards the guardians?"), and it has been the central theme in all subsequent programmed activities. From the first international NCLS conference, it was evident that similarities in professional duties and responsibilities that bound school leaders together cohesively were stronger than any differences arising from cultural and systemic contrasts (Williams, 1989).

From early exploratory activity, NCLS emerged as a regional forum for school practitioners and as an organization for sharing international experience among principals, headteachers, and others engaged in administration, teaching, or research in systemic reform. During the past decade more than one thousand participants have attended NCLS programs. Collectively, they represent an exceptionally broad range of experience and expertise from several countries, as school leaders, system administrators, university students and academics, governors and senators of provinces and states, national ministers of education, and other political representatives. The majority comes to Oxford from the United States, while others are from Africa, Australia, the Caribbean, Canada, the Czech Republic, Germany, India, Israel, and Poland. An international NCLS network of schools exists to promote school-to-school sharing of ideas, practitioner expertise, and faculty-student exchange visits.

To stimulate direct practitioner involvement, NCLS programs are essentially collaborative activities through practical, hands-on experience via school-focused networks. Explicit recognition of professional experience and expertise shared among school leaders as the main resource base for learning has been novel, invaluable, and affirming.

Typical of many observations on the NCLS "house style" is that of a UK headteacher: "It was not the impact made by leading national figures in education which enthused me, because there weren't any. . . . What most impressed me about the week's experience was the concept of bringing together headteachers . . . from this country with principals . . . from the USA and elsewhere and then creating conditions in which they learned from each other" (Tatlow, 1991).

Using this model, we have found that five recurrent themes have dominated NCLS international activities among school leaders during the past decade:

1. Systemic organization
2. Teaching and learning: frameworks and processes
3. Parental support and social importance
4. Reciprocal relationship: two-way traffic
5. Research activity

Systemic organization

At Oxford meetings, many U.S. principals find that differences among states are almost as great as those between the United Kingdom and their own systems. An enduring similarity is that every school system is immersed in rapid change, leading to identical practitioner concerns, such as central versus local political control, severe financial constraints, externally prescribed teaching and learning strategies, political tensions over school choice, and parental support for schools (Krueger, 1996).

Inevitably, comparisons between countries emerge in discussion. Although goal requirements in systemic education reforms are remarkably similar, the thrust of reform and improvement in student achievement in, for example, the United Kingdom and Israel has come via central government directives, whereas in the United States reform has been one element in consensual political vision shared among states (Casile, 1994).

A unique characteristic of systemic reform in the United Kingdom is that all publicly funded schools are now self-governing, with responsibility and accountability for the quality of educational provision shared between the professional staff and an elected board of governors. Each school has its own board of governors, which undertakes many of the functions of small-scale U.S. school districts and reflects the interests of parents, teachers, the LEA, and other local community representation. Each board is legally required to secure educationally effective and efficient provision. To achieve these goals, school governors have financial autonomy within nationally prescribed budgetary formulae, responsibility for appointment of teachers and support personnel, accountability for delivery of the national curriculum, and the task of monitoring and determining the exercise of parental choice (Williams, 1997a). To experience the impact of these sweeping reforms, NCLS has provided opportunities for overseas practitioners, administrators, and academics to visit schools and meet with their counterparts in the United Kingdom. Immediate comparisons and contrasts are visible in the relative sizes of schools and facilities provided. For example, compared with norms in North America, United Kingdom schools are small. Many have student enrollments of one hundred to two hundred students at primary and between seven hundred and eleven hundred at secondary schools. Average class sizes in the United Kingdom are larger than in North America: thirty to thirty-five is usual in primary and twenty-five to thirty in secondary schools. Similar averages for class sizes are not uncommon in Israel, the Czech Republic, and Poland.

It is universally acknowledged that in the United Kingdom introduction of self-governing schools has more fully realized the concepts of site-based management than in any other education system. Principals and academics from Poland and the Czech Republic have come to NCLS meetings mainly to study UK experience and mechanisms of local management of schools. For Israel, the United Kingdom system of self-governing schools is directly and immediately relevant to principals and central office administrators as the government has launched a site-based management project in several primary schools. Since 1992, Israeli educators have visited the NCLS network of schools and shared details of progress in Israel with other international participants at St. Peter's College, Oxford (Bar Eli, 1994). Most of the elementary school principals within Israel's innovative project have attended NCLS residential programs at Oxford.

Of considerable interest to international participants has been the devolution of self-governance to every publicly funded UK school. Accordingly, partnerships between schools and the communities they serve are visible through the functions and responsibilities of school governing bodies (Williams, 1995). Through direct experience in schools, visiting practitioners have returned to their own schools with greater awareness of their systemic and professional strengths together with an appreciation of possibilities for further development.

Under these conditions, practitioners quickly recognize the close similarities of their responsibilities and duties. One British educator neatly summarized the value of experiential perception: "How to reconcile the 'What' of teaching with the 'How' it is to be done is a shared concern . . . how to assess children in a way which makes the education system legitimately accountable to its community of parents and tax payers, without reducing the subtle process of children's learning to a set of numbers which undervalues the achievements of some, while labeling others as failures" (Potter, 1991).

Teaching and learning: frameworks and processes

The government's 1989 pantechnicon of prescribed curricula and assessment processes for schools in England and Wales began with a phased introduction of the national curriculum. The interventionist policy prescribed a core curriculum (English, mathematics, and science) and a foundation curriculum (history, geography, technology, art, music, a modern foreign language, and physical education). During NCLS annual international meetings, participants visit schools and experience the acclaimed UK tradition of learning by, rather than the teaching of, students. Without exception, self-directed learning is perceived as "children . . . taking responsibility for their own learning and decision making. The concepts of learning by doing and the belief that the classroom was not preparation for life but life itself were evident all around me" (Zelen, 1994).

During a decade of visits, workshops, and experience in classrooms, the main recurrent observations about UK schools have been identified:

• Teachers inventively use many resources to stimulate the development of creative thinking skills within frameworks of cooperative learning. Planned activities encourage students to become independent learners. There is a striking absence of the kind of textbooks typically distributed to students in the United States. Initially, some visitors are unsettled by the dearth of student textbooks. For others, it provides liberating insights: "When I asked students in an upper-junior-level English school to show me their textbooks, they were confounded. . . . 'Of course,' they told me, 'we have books.' But the concept of a single book for each discipline was missing. Classrooms are well stocked with books of various kinds, but each child does not possess the textbooks an American student is issued each year—science, spelling, math, social studies, handwriting, reading and English. . . . How wonderful it would be to organize instruction in a developmental hands-on way so that such books wouldn't be needed" (Locke, 1990).

• A common perception of classroom organization is that, although it is very different, it is progressively invigorating. Individual student desks have not been used in UK schools for many years. Usually, students sit in groups at tables and work collaboratively on projects and assignments under the direction of class teachers. In assigned activities, students usually work in small groups.

• Learning processes, either through oral discussion or by recording practical work, are stimulating. Through classroom displays of student work in written and graphic forms, genuine pride and enthusiasm in shared achievement is evident among learners. A further sense of collaborative achievement is evident when students speak confidently and clearly about concepts, problems, and solutions in their daily learning experiences.

• Similarly, the physical environment of classrooms provides positive experiences for visitors to UK schools. In most schools, multimedia techniques and three-dimensional forms are used to integrate collaborative class projects. One recollection typifies memories of school visits: "The halls and classrooms of the British schools were galleries of art and work! One could hardly walk down the hall for wanting to look at the fabric displays by the teachers and the work of the children. In the US . . . the local fire marshal prohibits teachers from hanging up the children's work in the hallways and classrooms. I'm wondering when the last elementary school burned down . . . ? I've lived there sixteen years and I can't remember one fire!" (McDowell, 1996).

Parental support and social importance

For many visitors, perceptions of parental support are tangible, a reinforcing and affirming influence of the importance of enduring partnerships between home and schools. At one primary school in Oxford, Weinman (1994) noted that students created their own set of rules for classroom behavior. Parents were expected to support both their children and the school through accepting and agreeing with their decisions.

Unfailingly, the UK tradition of everyone lunching in the school's dining area provides an unanticipated and pleasant surprise for visitors. A significant perception of the social importance of these occasions is evident through taking lunch together in classroom groups or "families," with older students assuming responsibility for well-mannered individual behavior within groups.

Reciprocal relationship: two-way traffic

Since 1990, a major NCLS activity has been the organization of ten-day biennial study group visits to the United States for UK headteachers and central office personnel. Efficiently programmed by generous colleagues in U.S. universities, visits have been made to Georgia (twice); Virginia; Long Island, New York; New Mexico (twice); and western Pennsylvania (twice). Organized around a two-center schedule, each visit has been invaluable in providing opportunities for direct learning experiences in schools about similarities and differences among education systems, school cultures, and differentiated levels of provision. UK groups have been graciously hosted by U.S. colleagues with whom they have gone to school each day to visit classes, experience diurnal patterns of school schedules and principals' duties, and absorb cultures of schools and neighborhoods.

Unsurprisingly, these activities have led to reciprocal links between schools; subsequent exchanges of curriculum schedules and learning materials; teacher and student correspondence; visiting programs; and, for some, shared family vacations. Collaborative activity exists between school faculties and students in Gloucestershire, Northamptonshire, and Oxfordshire and schools on Long Island and in Georgia, New Mexico, Pennsylvania, Virginia, Israel, and Poland. Exchange visits between teachers and student groups have followed from links forged between headteachers and principals either in Oxford or during NCLS group study visits. The benefits of professional contact, increasingly confident dialogue about curricular and role-alike responsibilities, and sharing of mutual experience by way of visiting each other's schools represent significant achievement by schools during the past decade, mainly through increased understanding among school leaders.

Research activity

Since its inception, NCLS has undertaken studies on practitioner leadership in schools. In addition to the dissemination of good practice in the running of schools, the Centre undertakes research into changing concepts of leadership. The main foci are "the centrality of core values essential in *earned* educational leadership status among 'followers'" (Williams, 1989). Essentially, NCLS studies emphasize the importance "for principals and headteachers to recognize . . . ways in which *others* in schools undertake . . . earned personal and professional leadership roles . . . to create communities of leaders" (Williams, 1989). The theme of the initial NCLS international conference was "The School as a Community of Leaders," a leitmotiv that has developed consistently since 1989. Subsequent studies indicate that in various schools leaders and followers are working collaboratively and confidently in their earned roles. Awareness of reciprocal relationships between "leaders and followers clearly indicate[s] that both sets of roles are interdependent, complementary and elective" (Williams, 1997b). Explicit recognition that the roles are neither competitive nor submissive invariably leads to providing new opportunities for professional development that offer experience and training for "succession" in an earned leadership school culture.

Future international sharing and reflection

Following a decade of continuous activity and development, experiences for hands-on practitioners within the NCLS network have led to positive and informed outcomes. Through mandated reform in many international systems, schools, communities, teachers, and students have endured remarkably similar problems—initiated mainly by governmental decisions. Although political solutions applied to educational problems are unique to each system and culture, participants in programs at St. Peter's College have been acutely aware that teachers and administrators in schools have to interpret and respond to mandated policy-in-action reform programs, intended to produce immediate benefit to students and in the longer term to the communities and nations they serve. The keen blade of systemic reform is most incisive at the school level. It is in schools that "value-laden terms such as 'citizenship,' 'access,' 'equity,' 'inclusion,' and 'education as investment' are perceived, experienced, reality-tested, and assessed" (Alexander and Williams, 1992).

Recognition of the similarity of inherent effects in education reform processes has helped an international fraternity of school leaders to share immutable democratic educational values. In turn, through reflecting on shared concerns they become aware of ways in which solutions to problems might be formulated and difficulties overcome. It is through such mutual perception and sharing that sustained international collaboration may be justified. First, an awareness of similarities and differences in societal expectations and educational priorities in other systems is consciously realized. Second, informed awareness leads to further exploration and calibration of similarities and differences within one's own culture. Third, insight into other education systems leads to clarification of issues as well as an inventory of possible options—frequently on a basis of "adopt, adapt, improve, own."

In 1900, the distinguished British educator Sir Michael Sadler asserted that "the practical value of studying in a right spirit . . . the working of foreign systems of education is that it will result in our being better fitted to study and understand our own" (Higginson, 1980). In endorsement of Sadler's assertion, the Norham Centre for Leadership Studies at Oxford has provided a collaborative experiential forum for school leaders from diverse education systems. Additionally, through its research activities NCLS is engaged in studies on the practice of distributed leadership in schools.

Arising from a decade of NCLS international activities, the central focus for further development continues to be provision of opportunities for school leaders to clarify and affirm that authentic leadership in schools is a status that has to be *earned* from the colleagues, students, parents, and local communities they serve.

References

Alexander, K., and Williams, V. (eds.). *Reforming Education in a Changing World*. Blacksburg, Va.: JEF, 1992.

Bar Eli, D. "Developments in Israel's Site-Based Management Policy Initiatives." NCLS *Conference Reflections*, 1994.

Casile, W. J. "I Travelled to Oxford: A Kindred Journey." NCLS *Conference Reflections*, 1994.

Higginson, J. H. *Selections from Michael Sadler*. Liverpool, England: Dejall and Meyorre, 1980.

Krueger, J. A. "An Experience in Transformational Learning." NCLS *Conference Reflections*, 1996.

Locke, J. "Longing for Simplicity." NCLS *Conference Reflections*, 1990.

Maclure, J. S. *Education Reformed*. London, England: Hodder and Stoughton, 1989.

McDowell, C. "I Saw the 'Forest' While Visiting Oxford." NCLS *Conference Reflections*, 1996.

Potter, D. "Priorities." NCLS *Conference Reflections*, 1991.

Tatlow, J. "The Oxford Experience." NCLS *Conference Reflections*, 1991.

Weinman, B. "The Oxford Trip." NCLS *Summer Institute Reflections*, 1994.

Williams, V. "Postscript: The End of the Beginning." NCLS *Conference Reflections*, 1989.

Williams, V. *Towards Self-Managing Schools.* London, England: Cassell, 1995.

Williams, V. "School Autonomy and Parental Choice: Circumscribed Realities of Reform." In R. Shapira and P. Cookson (eds.), *Autonomy and Choice in Context: An International Perspective.* New York: Pergamon/Elsevier Science, 1997a.

Williams, V. "School Leadership: New Expectations." *Network NEWS-NOTES*, 1997b, *11* (1).

Zelen, P. "Enduring Oxford Impressions." NCLS *Summer Institute Reflections*, 1994.

VIVIAN WILLIAMS *is a fellow in education at St. Peter's College, University of Oxford, director of the Norham Centre for Leadership Studies, and a research fellow for the Leverhulme Trust from 1997 to 1999.*

Key to our growth as individuals within our community of learners are the relationships we have with one another. We have found this true in our workplaces, both for ourselves and others. The author shares the lessons she's learned about relationships from her years of experience in principals' centers.

5

Relationships

Gayle Moller

WHEN ANYONE asks a local real estate office what makes a difference in the selling price of a home, the well-known answer is, "Location, location, location." In building a professional development center for school leaders, success relies on relationships, relationships, relationships. Our Center evolved by paying attention to layers upon layers of relationships.

Relationships start a center

The idea of our South Florida Center for Educational Leaders was launched twelve years ago by an elementary principal who returned from a principals' summer institute at Vanderbilt University. She walked into the district HRD office and expressed the awe she had felt by being in such a rich learning environment in that institute. Then she questioned why this type of experience couldn't happen in South Florida. Why not?

A small group of school leaders started meeting informally at a local park. The meetings were comfortable, but we soon realized

NEW DIRECTIONS FOR SCHOOL LEADERSHIP, NO. 7, SPRING 1998 © JOSSEY-BASS PUBLISHERS

that to succeed we needed a sustaining structure. Three colleagues met to discuss the possibilities and then decided to pull others together to plan. Before the meeting, we recruited two credible principals to attend the Annual Conversation of the International Network of Principals' Centers to gather data to share.

The people who came to our organizational meeting represented school-based and district administrators from across South Florida. We had high expectations. Everyone was polite, the administrators who had attended the Conversation shared, discussions followed, and then we watched a ceiling of indifference appear within the room. The idea of a center was alien to most of the participants. They had no experience to draw from in trying to understand the idea. After the meeting, the planners gathered to commiserate. But we weren't willing to give up.

LESSON LEARNED: *The wrong people attended the meeting. Many lacked experience to join in the vision of a center. The relationships were not established.*

Relationships ensure resources

The next fall, we invited the superintendent from each of the five school systems in our area to send a principal and a district administrator to a two-day planning retreat. This time we carefully recommended like-minded individuals who could understand the concept of a center. A skillful facilitator helped us work through the possibilities and obstacles. With a shared vision and an incentive of possible state funding, we agreed to move forward. An action plan was developed for members of the group to meet with their respective superintendents to share a position paper describing our ideas and seek their support.

The action plan succeeded, but with a caveat. The superintendents made it clear that their school systems would not provide funds for the Center. We could seek state funding with their endorsement, but we could not expect financial support from the school districts. At the time we were pleased to have their support to apply for state funds. We felt as long as we had base funding, the rest could be established. After ten years, we now realize that to be dependent on one source of funding is unwise.

LESSON LEARNED: Build relationships that lead to multiple sources of funding. Reliance on a single source places a center in a tenuous position. If the advocate for funding leaves, the center is placed in jeopardy.

Relationships sustain self

The board of directors for the new Center recruited an outstanding administrator who agreed to leave her school district to assume leadership of the Center. The new director's strength was her interpersonal skills; she quickly engaged the board in planning events for the Center. We supported the new director and were enthusiastic at our meetings, but as we moved back into our day-to-day lives the memory of our commitments waned. She was left alone to build this ambiguous project called a center.

LESSON LEARNED: As well-meaning as board members are, the labor rests with the professional staff. Members of the board do not think about the future of the Center with the same intensity as the staff does. Even after ten years of building a strong board of directors, execution of the mission is left to the staff. As current director, I accept this isolation and, at times, even appreciate the autonomy, but the lack of close relationships to carry out the work saps the energy of even the most dedicated person.

Relationships establish broad networks

After one year, the first director returned to her home district to assume a principalship, which was her personal goal. I was then selected to lead the Center. I found that to effectively lead I had to reach out for meaningful relationships. In my case, the first resources came from members of the International Network of Principals' Centers. Gordy Donaldson, Roland Barth, Scotty Scott, and others recognized a struggling soul and reached out to support the Center's efforts. Then Dennis Sparks, executive director of the National Staff Development Council, shared with me the difficulties his organization experienced.

LESSON LEARNED: *There are amazing resources throughout the country waiting to be tapped. As large as this country is, we draw close through these connections. A telephone call or an e-mail conversation can make the work less lonely and let you know that what you are doing is important.*

Relationships advance adult learning

By accepting state funding, our Center became one of five state regional service agencies. Since the primary funding was from the state department of education, there were obligations. The agenda became school improvement. The five regional directors worked well together and developed state-of-the-art professional development for school leaders.

This was the beginning of the school improvement movement within our state, and in the past the adults in the schools rarely worked together to achieve goals. As a new center, we used these programs as an opportunity to build relationships across a large urban region. The programs were content-driven, but we paid attention to activities that would help people reveal their beliefs about education in a relatively risk-free setting. Celebrations, conversations, raucous skits, and genuine emotions were honored. Most programs extended from three to nine months. Groups met for three or more multiday sessions. This approach helped people make meaning out of the urgency to reform schools.

Educators from Key West were bonding with colleagues from Palm Beach. Some of these friendships still exist today and provide safety for candid talk about their fears, concerns, and successes.

Memories were built through humor and sadness. For example, Hurricane Andrew devastated our region only three weeks after the initial retreat of our first leadership series. Almost half of our participants suffered loss from the storm. Our staff was certain that the program would end right there because people had to deal with their survival needs. We contacted the administrators from the unaffected school districts and matched each one with a person who worked in the storm-strewn area. The schools and their leaders went to work providing support for their colleagues. When we met only a month after the storm, everyone was there. One participant told us that attending the meeting meant she was assured of sleeping in a clean room, so she came thankfully.

Education is complex, and school leaders often feel guilty that they don't know the answers. Whenever the Center provides learning experiences that affirm their beliefs and the "experts" support those beliefs, they feel more confident. They're OK. If that learning occurs within a group of people they respect and enjoy, the learning is even more significant.

LESSON LEARNED: If we paid attention to the emotional needs of our members, they came back to learn more. The investment in these activities opened their minds to learning about themselves and their schools.

Relationships build capacity

If the Center were to survive, it was necessary to build a core membership that believed in the work we were doing. Most of these people were participants in the long-term programs we offered. They developed relationships among themselves and wanted to continue their connections. Opportunities to sustain these relationships and build the capacity of leadership within the Center emerged from the members.

An example of this leadership resulted in the Center's hosting an Annual Conversation for the International Network of Principals' Centers. After attending the Conversation in Atlanta, the chairperson and chairperson-elect returned with a plan. They announced that they were going to recruit a group to go to Sitka, Alaska, for the next Conversation. At first, this seemed improbable, but they did it. With a single vision, they enlisted twenty people to join our adventure. The Center served as the facilitator of the arrangements, but the impetus came from these leaders.

In Alaska, the group volunteered our Center to host the 1996 Annual Conversation. As a result of their initiative, we continued to plan Conversation trips for the next two years, and in 1996 we were indeed the hosts. The steering committee served for two years and experienced the positive and negative emotions that groups predictably experience. Our staff worked in the background to facilitate logistics, learning, and other details. The success of the 1996 Conversation paralleled the enthusiasm and pride our members felt on the last day of the event. Volunteers stuffed name tags into holders, drove international guests to visit schools, stayed up all night to publish a memorable document, and missed participating in conversation sessions while creating a video to help guests capture their reflections.

LESSON LEARNED: What may appear as a wild idea can develop leadership capacity to advance a center. The people who contributed still talk with pride about their Annual Conversation. The Center staff needs to walk a few steps behind the leadership to allow the latter to emerge. The payoff for the future of a center is ongoing support in the most dire of circumstances.

Relationships protect the members

School districts may be hazardous to the health of school leaders. Stressful demands coming from many directions place people in the position of uncertainty as to what will be accepted by the larger system. Punishment comes in many forms in school systems. A comment from a line supervisor, or disapproval of personal plans for professional development, sends a message to members that the Center is not credible.

It is important to maintain positive relationships with the people having the potential to deliver these messages. Most want to support the *personnel* within the school district, but without enough information it is easy to be skeptical about programs that pull people from the schools. To maintain these relationships, in our Center we use small acts that keep our name in front of these decision makers; an example is sending a newspaper clipping about a program that a supervisor developed. Also, handwritten cards are sent as informal messages that are more likely to be read than printed materials.

Another strategy is to keep these important people informed about how the Center is professionally active. For example, offer to bring to the school district a person whose reputation is well known and who can help them address a district issue. By providing this resource, the Center becomes known as connected to the larger educational community. Another strategy is to publish articles about programs the Center sponsors as a way to legitimize the activities.

LESSON LEARNED: *Because the Center is an external agency to large school systems, district leaders can easily dismiss it and its contributions. They need reminders about how the Center makes their work easier and helps them meet their goals. The strategies may be subtle, or they may use flashing lights that say, "This is a good place to allow your people to learn." Regardless of how this is accomplished, neglecting to do so may find members gradually moving away from the Center because their supervisors, consciously or unconsciously, let them know it is not valuable.*

Relationships maintain the momentum

In the early years, we thought it would be prudent to have a strategic plan. We found the most valuable part of the process was the struggle to develop our beliefs and mission. Even though they have been amended over the years, they are fundamentally the same.

The mission of the Center is to serve educational leaders and to influence change that results in improved educational outcomes by providing learning opportunities in a trusting, supportive, and collegial environment.

The mission is based upon these beliefs:

- Sharing professional experiences benefits all.
- Learning throughout one's career is a professional responsibility.
- Together we know more than each of us does alone.
- Expectations influence expectations.
- Leaders need a safe, trusting environment for personal and professional renewal.
- Recognition and celebrations energize.
- Leaders have a responsibility to influence change in education.
- Education has a responsibility to serve the public interest.
- Collaboration between the public and private sectors fosters continuous educational improvement.

Acting on these beliefs, people come to Center events for relationship-based reasons:

- The exciting learning experience touches their sense of what is right.
- Their friends come.
- They have fun and laugh, while learning.
- They feel important being connected to high-level intellectual experiences.

LESSON LEARNED: A center needs to be driven by a solid belief system. Put aside the "guilt" of not being highly structured, in order to achieve goals. Be flexible within these beliefs.

Relationships prepare for the future

The Center started as an organization for school administrators. As schools engaged more teachers in decision making, the board debated who should make up the membership. After three years of discussion, they agreed to invite teachers to be members. The evolution of the Center to a more broad-based membership then challenged us to see the value of administrators and teachers learning together.

This inclusiveness led to formation of the South Florida Consortium of Schools, which began with twenty schools and, in its second year, now has forty-three schools as members. The school teams learn together and share resources. Although we strive to pursue an agenda of schoolwide action research about teaching and learning, the highest value voiced by the people who join us is attached to the relationships they develop during their time together.

The next stage of the Center is to challenge these pioneers to reflect seriously on their practice and adjust it to influence student growth. The luxury of networking solely to build relationships is in the past. As the public demands changes, educators must produce results from these relationships. The Consortium offers the safety to try strategies while building relationships within their schools and with other schools.

LESSON LEARNED: A major project such as the Consortium is built on past relationships. The idea would not have been accepted ten years ago. Only by drawing on relationships were we able to attract people to volunteer their time, funds, and energy to work toward substantive change.

Relationships help you say good-bye

The invitation to contribute to this volume was timely. My personal life is demanding a move to another state, which means away from the Center. It's been twelve years of dreaming, and now the time to say good-bye is here. Regardless of my plans to move, it is time for a different type of leadership. We study and talk about organizations, but living it forces us to face reality. The Center had a strong advocate for eight years who supported funding for the activities and allowed the programs to develop with few restraints.

The advocate retired, and funding from this source was discontinued. Three years ago we predicted this would happen and started a development program, but I am not the person to build this effort. A new leader will build relationships to expand the funding structure.

Losing a powerful advocate requires that a formal power structure protect the organization and ensure that funders see it as a viable program to support. We hope to find a "home" within an institution of higher learning. The most important asset the Center brings is the relationships built over the last ten years. We believe this will be recognized and seized as an opportunity to expand a university's outreach agenda. The other option is that the Center will become a memory of a ten-year period in South Florida when educators learned to work, laugh, and cry together while striving to make schools better for their students.

This reflection is powerful for me. Inevitably the memories come forth as I think about my own twelve-year adventure. Questions about my leadership emerge as I reflect. What could I have done differently to make the Center more able to sustain itself? Did my leadership style keep us from becoming a more recognizable entity to attract funding? How could I have encouraged more leadership from the members? Did I try to do too much myself and not capitalize on the talent eager to contribute? These are questions I take with me and hopefully learn from to enrich my next adventure. For certain, I know we needed relationships to make it happen.

GAYLE MOLLER *is executive director of the South Florida Center for Educational Leaders in Davis.*

One of the most precious gifts we find in the Network is the spiritual connection that remains with us despite geographic distances. The author truly understands and reminds us of the importance of this both in our daily work and whenever we're in one another's presence. Listen in as he shares his thoughts about the origin, nature, and value of these connections.

6

Harbor Lights Cafe

David Hagstrom

GREAT IDEAS come to me like gentle doves. I hear their faint fluttering most clearly when in conversation with a friend. My "big ideas" (even my modest awakenings and little understandings) don't come as a result of a lecture or being taught. In fact, my most significant learnings about myself seem to catch me most unexpectedly when I'm captured completely in thoughts about another's life and that person's needs and necessities. It's within conversation that my personal truths and the possibilities of future victories come to me.

Twenty years ago, Roland Barth and I had our first conversation. It was in December 1977, and I had just read an article Roland wrote for *The Elementary Principal.* The article was entitled "Take a Cord of Red Oak . . . Reflections on Not Being a School Principal." Roland wrote that article while on sabbatical from the Newton, Massachusetts, public schools. He wrote his words about the "constant worries of the principalship" while spending a year away from his responsibilities at his beloved farm, secluded near the village of Head Tide in Maine. I read that article while at our farm,

NEW DIRECTIONS FOR SCHOOL LEADERSHIP, NO. 7, SPRING 1998 © JOSSEY-BASS PUBLISHERS

secluded near the village of Green Lake, Wisconsin. I was a principal at the Willard School in Evanston, Illinois, and used the Wisconsin farm as a getaway from my stressful and anxiety-filled days as an elementary school principal. As a result of reading Roland's reflections about spending a year away from his work, I made an immediate and heartfelt connection with this kindred New England spirit. I first wrote to Roland, thanking him for writing the words that helped me understand why I tossed and turned so during the course of my work. Then I gave him my phone number at Meadowood Farm and asked whether he would be willing to call me so that we could begin talking about the frustrations we seemed to hold in common. In December 1977, Roland called me. Since that time, we've had conversations off Round Pond in Maine, aboard a ferryboat in Alaska, in countless taverns across the country, and of course at the Harvard Principals' Center.

Becky van der Bogert, Richard Ackerman, and Gordon Donaldson have been my friends for just about as long as I've known Roland. I met them all "in conversation." The first recollection I have of being in conversation with Becky was when I was on sabbatical at Harvard. I remember feeling so fortunate to be at Harvard during the early days of the Principals' Center and at the birthing of the International Network of Principals' Centers. I remember being a part of a particularly joyous conversation one day at Gutman Library when it seemed we almost effortlessly hatched the idea of creating the Network. Born amid laughter and storytelling was an idea that literally kept me in professional balance wherever I was to roam over the next few years.

I remembered that day later as I took part in creating the North Suburban Principals' Center in Chicago. I remembered that day as I took part in creating the Rural School Leadership Network in Fairbanks. I remembered that day as I took part in creating Alaska's Center for Educational Leadership. And I remember that day as now I take part in creating a new Principals' Center in Oregon. On that day in Cambridge, now some time ago, Becky said to me, "We'll be fast friends from now on, David. No matter what circumstances, we can count on this friendship to carry us through life's major difficulties." It's been so true. Whether at Wingspread, in Sitka, or wherever, Becky and I have cherished our conversations about job changes, cancer surgery, or whatever. Parts of an ill-remembered poem come to my mind as I recall my conversations with Becky: "because she cared, she heard; because she heard, she often healed without words."

The conversation I remember most vividly with Richard was held outside the Conference Center in Green Bay, Wisconsin. We talked about Parker Palmer and his sense of a need for a new movement among educators (akin to the civil rights movement). We talked "the way of the movement," where isolated individuals decide to stop leading divided lives and discover each other forming groups for mutual support. We discussed for hours the notion that as a movement grows, the affirmation one does not receive from organizational colleagues is received from friends within the movement. I remember that conversation so clearly because I've felt for years that I've been a part of a movement, and the affirmation I've needed has come constantly—from Richard! On that day in Green Bay, and during every conversation Richard and I have ever had, we end our time with the Quaker phrase, "The way will open." The way has been continuously opening for me. Thanks, Richard, for your constant presence. You bring me to solid ground.

Throughout all the years I was in Alaska, Gordon Donaldson was my balance at the other end of the continent. "Alaska and Maine have so many similarities," we'd often tell one another. Of course, this was true. Climate. Weather. Temperament. Hockey frenzy! But to tell the real truth, the commonalities of our two pieces of geography were small potatoes compared to our personal passions and causes: baseball for one, and love of family for another. Gordy, just the thought of your smile and laughter, one conversation after another, got me through countless snowstorms and many a "forty below."

These conversations with my friends have informed my work at leadership centers across the nation. My conversations with Roland, Becky, Richard, and Gordy have provided the strong foundation work that makes it possible for me to invite others into conversation with one another, in Illinois, in Alaska, and now in Oregon. The spirited and spiritual connections I have with Roland, Becky, Richard, and Gordy have made possible spirited and spiritual connections among hundreds of educators they've never met. My work is very much the result of the "constant presence" of my old-time friends from the Network. Watch them at work in *my* work.

My initial principals' center work came as a result of a telephone call from Dick Streedain, then a principal in Glenview, Illinois. I was the principal at Willard School in Evanston at the time Dick called me. As I recall that phone call, now almost twenty years ago, it went something like this: "David, mutual friends have suggested that we get together for a conversation. They say that we think alike about our work. Let's have a meal together soon." I said that I'd like that a lot, and that I'd bring along a poem. When we met the next week, I brought "Two Tramps in Mudtime," by Robert Frost. For me the poem was all about the process of finding meaning in our work:

But yield who will to their separation,
My object in living is to unite
My avocation and my vocation
As my two eyes make one in sight.
Only where love and need are one,
And the work is play for mortal stakes,
Is the deed ever really done
For Heaven and the future's sakes.

Dick liked the poem, and wanted to know whether I'd read particular books by Elizabeth O'Connor, Henri Nouwen, Robert Raines, and Carl Sandburg. I said that I had. With the surprising awareness that we'd devoured all the same books, we launched into a three-hour conversation that centered on how we must connect with the best parts of who we are, and that when we do so we'll know what motivates us in our work. Our conversation that night ended with a Robert Raines quote: "When the energy of inner necessity yields clarity in the center of the soul, ambivalence gives birth to vocation." I remember saying, "Wow, I want to hang around this guy a lot!"

We did hang around together a lot . . . for many years, in fact. During the course of our conversations, we wondered if other principals in the Chicago area might appreciate the opportunity to explore "the meaning of our work," and might need the chance to tell "war stories" out of school (so to speak). We started with the two of us, but before long we were meeting regularly with scores of other north suburban principals. Early on, we realized that conversations about our work came more easily if we met in a setting identified as a "safe harbor." Perhaps it was time spent with colleagues at the North Suburban Principals' Center that got me to thinking: as principals we need so desperately to be in some really safe place to talk about our work.

Then my work took me to Alaska. It was exciting. My work took me to so many out-of-the-way places, to almost all of the small villages, in fact. I met outstanding principals and principal teachers as a result of my university administrator preparation activities. Not too surprisingly, Alaskan educators needed to find meaning in their work. They, too, needed to investigate their motivations and understandings in the relaxing atmosphere of some "safe place." Countless Alaskan educators suggested to me that they needed time away to think about their work. Jack Clark, a principal at a small village near Bethel, spoke for many when he said, "We want an arena for interacting personally about those things that concern us professionally." As a result of conversations with Jack and his many colleagues in the rural villages, Alaska's Rural School Leadership Network was established at Fairbanks. The group met to better understand the work of a school leader in village Alaska, and to encourage the group's members to better understand themselves. During the course of our conversations, we created a sort of mythical "Harbor Lights Cafe." Later, after I became a principal in Alaska, I cherished the special meeting times that became our place away.

While in Alaska, I often felt that my every worry and concern would be solved by the presence of a Harbor Lights Cafe. As a principal on my own storm-tossed ocean, I would often think of the HL Cafe, and I'd smile. You see, the mere presence in my mind of a place of hospitality, warmth, understanding, reassurance, and inspiration moved me forward and gave me hope.

I know that this cafe longing began years ago (while on sabbatical at the Harvard Principals' Center, in fact), as I sat among lobster fishermen at the Driftwood Cafe in Marblehead, Massachusetts. After days of hard labor, stormy times, and tough isolation, these fisherfolk came together, having weathered the storm. They were strongly joyous as they shared words from the sea, prepared to mend their nets, and tuned in intently to listen to some fellow tell his story of the way it will be *next time.*

Isolation, worry, and concern. They blended with creativity and exhilaration . . . and these words pretty well summarize my years as a principal in Alaska. The words all rang true with my colleagues as well. But the words missing in our professional lives were those I found among the Marblehead fishermen as they prepared to mend their nets. They shone forth like a beacon from the Driftwood Cafe: *Hospitality. Warmth. Understanding. Reassurance. Inspiration.*

As Alaskan educators, we elected to actually create a Harbor Lights Cafe. It represented what was missing in our professional-growth lives. We discovered that it was critical for us to get together regularly to share stories, to discover what help is and what it isn't, and to focus intently on the meaning of our work. We did so using conversations as a vehicle. We found that, time after time, conversations would bring us home . . . to who we were, and to who we wanted to be.

Yes, great ideas come in like gentle doves. We hear their faint fluttering best when in conversation with a friend. Now I'm in conversation with my friends here in Oregon. The idea that has quietly appeared over the last few weeks is that principals continue to need a Harbor Lights Cafe. In this location (Oregon), we're thinking that it will come in the form of a series of seminars to be called Leadership and Learning: Personal Change in a Professional Setting. The seminars will offer a context for participants to explore the difficult dilemmas we all experience in our work.

Each member of the seminar group will be responsible for investigating a particular issue or dilemma in that person's teaching or administrative life. We'll use Parker Palmer's "Clearness Committee" method to assist seminar participants in achieving greater clarity in their work. And we'll use conversations as our way of being one with the other. We'll attempt to be *totally attentive* to one another.

So: Roland, Becky, Richard, and Gordy, do you see continuances of our ongoing conversations in my work over the years? Do you see how the honest, open dialogue we've had with one another helps me be *totally attentive* to others, appreciating the stories we all have to share? Do you recognize yourselves in these stories?

Years ago, I read novels written by Anthony West. In *Heritage*, West described what conversation usually is and hinted at what it can be: "All my life I had lived alone, inside a wall of my own desires, inside the ghetto of my own demands for happiness. I had never seen anyone else's actions, or interpreted their words, unless it was through the veil of their effect on me. . . . When I talked, I discussed my own necessities: I had never had a conversation in which gifts of understanding and recognitions had been exchanged" (West, 1955).

Roland, Becky, Richard, and Gordy: "I had never had conversations in which gifts of understanding and recognitions had been exchanged . . ." until I participated in conversation with you. Because of these conversations with you, I have come close to discovering the center of my life in my own heart, and come closer, I believe, to helping others do the same. Thanks for encouraging me to encourage others. Thank you for assisting us all in this process of finding meaning in our work.

References

Barth, R. "Take a Cord of Red Oak . . . Reflections on Not Being a School Principal." *Elementary Principal,* Dec. 1977, pp. 6–7.

Frost, R. *Selected Poems of Robert Frost.* Austin, Tex.: Holt, Rinehart and Winston, 1967. From *The Poetry of Robert Frost,* edited by Edward Connery Lathem, Copyright 1936 by Robert Frost. © 1964 by Lesley Frost Ballantine. © 1969 by Henry Holt & Company. Reprinted by permission of Henry Holt and Company, Inc.

Nouwen, H. *Reaching Out.* New York: Doubleday, 1975.
O'Connor, E. *Our Many Selves.* New York: HarperCollins, 1971.
Palmer, P. "Divided No More: A Movement Approach to Educational Reform." *Change,* Mar./Apr. 1992, pp. 10–17.
Raines, R. *Going Home.* New York: HarperCollins, 1979.
Sandburg, C. *The People, Yes.* Orlando: Harcourt Brace, 1936.
West, A. *Heritage.* New York: Random House, 1955. © Random House, Inc. Used by permission.

DAVID HAGSTROM *is associate professor at Lewis and Clark College in Portland, Oregon, and deals with issues of school management and leadership. He is also the founder of New Viewpoint Educators, a consulting firm that specializes in assisting school groups in finding the shared vision that unite them in their work. He is in the process of writing a book,* Stories That Make Our Hearts Sing.

One of the rich pieces of the Network is ongoing conversation among professors of educational administration and practitioners, bridging theory and practice. The author of this chapter had the courage to give up his role as professor completely and return to a school to see if he could "walk his talk." Listen to his story.

7

Back to School

Joe A. Richardson

IT WAS THE Friday morning prior to Labor Day weekend, 1990. Typical for this time of the year, it was already very warm and only 8:00 A.M. This was my first day as head of a small, progressive independent school of some 530 students, ages two through eighteen. As I was about to examine my calendar to plan my day's activities, the lights went out and all electrical power was off. Within five minutes, the head custodian appeared to inform me that the school's transformer had blown up. He reported that during the summer months fifteen new room air conditioners had been installed, and apparently the load was too much for the transformer. This being the Friday before a holiday, it was his judgment that it would be impossible to get an electrician to do the necessary work, and even if we could, there was no way we could secure a new transformer before the following Tuesday, the day classes were to begin.

So this is what it means to be back in school.

My journey back to school started some thirty-four years ago in a small midwestern city. I began teaching mathematics and science

NEW DIRECTIONS FOR SCHOOL LEADERSHIIP, NO. 7, SPRING 1998 © JOSSEY-BASS PUBLISHERS in grades seven and eight. The community was made up of hard-working, middle-class people; it was an area I knew well, having lived a few miles away in a small railroad town across the Mississippi River. I wore my new thirty-five-dollar suit, my shoes were shined, and I was ready! My classes were all about the same size, twenty-five to thirty students. My lesson plans were in order, and I remembered the sound words of advice from my critic teacher: "Start out tough; you can always loosen up later."

It was during my inaugural parent conference that I received the first informal assessment of my teaching effectiveness. This particular mother looked at her son's folder and then looked me right in the eye and said, "Billy sure ain't learning nothing in here." She went on to inform me that she was doing her part; Billy's homework was always checked and she made sure he was never late for school. She wanted to know why I had not done my part. Pretty straightforward, no dancing around, a simple fact: the teacher had made no impact whatsoever on her son.

Then there was Tom. My first attempt at continuous progress instruction involved organizing worksheets in mathematics that would be progressively more difficult. Students could work at their own pace and come to me to have their work checked. Tom brought me two papers he wanted checked. As I looked at them, I noticed he had done the same worksheet twice. When asked if he realized it, he looked at the papers and responded, "That's funny, because I didn't get any of the same answers."

I taught in that community for five years. Our principal was a no-nonsense disciplinarian who also had a most delightful sense of humor. He was open, fair, and committed to the well-being of all members of the school community. Although he believed a regulation was meant to be respected, his first concern was for the child. He evaluated me on a regular basis, which meant that he visited my class regularly and within an hour after the visit a copy of his report was in my mailbox. Those five years established for me the fact that I wanted to remain in education. Furthermore, I found life with thirteen- and fourteen-year-olds was very interesting. In some sense, they were like first graders; they would try anything and accept most any challenge. In turn, they challenged me not only as an instructor of mathematics and science but also on the human level. They would test me to find out how I would behave if my views were challenged. Often, as a twenty-two-year-old, I exhibited behavior similar to theirs; I would be defensive and respond in ways that didn't reflect much maturity. Perhaps more than anything else, I learned that I had as much control over our environment as they were willing to give me.

My next stop was in a school district on the North Shore of Chicago. This was a much different setting, an upper-middle-class community, confident and well educated. It was in this setting I learned something about "involved parents," meaning that they were demanding and used to getting their way. After three years of teaching and three more years in supervisory roles, I was appointed principal of the new middle school. Here I had my first real experience with talented, confident teachers and what it was like to work with strong faculty. After one of our faculty meetings, our mathematics coordinator, a woman of immense talent and a reputation for deflating egos, stormed into my office and proceeded to play back for me my performance at our faculty meeting. She folded her arms across her chest, commenced pacing back and forth repeating, with devastating effect, some of the less-than-useful phrases I had made to the faculty. She concluded her performance with "And who do you think you are?" I came to cherish this relationship. I had my first real experience with "tough love." She never held grudges, and once the message was delivered it was over.

We were in the process of constructing a new building on our campus. The architect and the contractor gave us a schedule that would allow us to move into our new building during the late fall, prior to really cold weather. In one sense, they were correct. We were able to move into the building without fear of really cold weather. We moved in March. March in Illinois is a time of the year when temperatures vary between 30 and 50 degrees. It is also the time when it snows, rains, freezes, and thaws. It provided thirteen- and fourteen-year-old youngsters with a new way to challenge the adults in their lives. There was a large mound of dirt near the newly completed building, which soon became a large pile of mud. Our students were mesmerized by it, which produced a custodian's nightmare. By necessity each and every student, prior to entering the new building, had to walk through it.

After nine years on the North Shore, I accepted an appointment as a member of the department of educational administration at Georgia State University, in the heart of downtown Atlanta. For the next twenty years, this was my workplace. It was an emerging institution driven largely by a city that was growing at an alarming rate. As a member of the educational administration department, I was responsible for helping prepare principals for their work in the public schools of Georgia. Coming from a middle-school setting where teachers taught five hours every day, I looked forward to the prospect of teaching two courses a week.

The years at the university were enjoyable and for the most part quite satisfying. I had the opportunity to watch our two children grow up, attend their functions, and actually be a part of their lives. There were opportunities to become involved in some interesting professional activities, one of which was working with the Schools of Excellence Program, which originated in the U.S. Office of Education. As a site visitor in this program, I was responsible for visiting schools around the country. On one of my visits, I arrived in town a day early. Since the school was quite close to the motel, I decided I would try out the running track. As I entered the track from a side gate, I noticed a security guard, who appeared to be running in my direction. As he approached he began shouting at me to remain where I was and not to move. He asked me if I could read; I replied that I could. Apparently there were some signs near the main entrance announcing the track was off limits while repairs were being completed. Furthermore, he said that I must accompany him to the principal's office and explain in person why I had ignored the directive. The guard took me straight to the principal's office and proudly announced to the principal that he had caught me violating a school regulation. The principal dismissed the guard, apologized for the treatment I had received, and suggested a running course nearby. I decided not to tell him why I was in town.

The next morning, I appeared in his office, reintroduced myself, and told him my reason for being there. His mouth dropped open, he fell back into his chair, put his head down on the desk, and remained in that position for a couple of minutes. No amount of reassurance from me could bring color back to his face. His school was a very healthy place for students, faculty, and parents. He was known to be an excellent teacher and leader, much loved by his community. I am sure he did not fully recover until he received notice that his school had been selected as a school of excellence.

During my first year at the university, one of my students suggested that I accompany her to the school where she was principal of the primary unit. She believed it represented the kind of school we had conceptualized during our class meetings. The Galloway School, an independent school of about five hundred students, was located in a city park on the north side of the city. It was diverse racially, ethnically, economically, and academically. There were no grade levels, no letter grades were used in evaluation, and although there were three units to the school (early learning, middle learning, and upper learning), the boundaries between the units were very much blurred. My first impression of the school was that it was very disorganized and chaotic.

I was introduced to the headmaster, Elliott Galloway. He was familiar with the school system where I had been a principal. Galloway was very well read, and much of what he talked about seemed to come from his study of Dewey. He invited me to visit as often as possible. Over the years, Galloway and I became good friends. He is a great storyteller. Metaphors, parables, and sea stories were and continue to be his instruments of communication. He told me how, as a former naval officer, a Baptist minister, and a former principal of a middle school, he came to start his own school. In 1969, when both public and private schools in Atlanta were experiencing confusion about how to realign schools to meet the new court ordered desegregation mandates, he decided it was time to start his own school. So with seventy-three cents and a short-term lease on a condemned county-owned old folks home, he opened his school, a racially integrated school for students ages two through eighteen—a school he would lead for the next twenty-two years.

In the mid-1970s, Galloway asked me to participate in a study that was being conducted by a regional accrediting agency. Our committee's first visit to the school was in February; it was unusually cold by Atlanta standards. On the second day of our four-day visit, the ancient furnace in the 1911 building ceased to function. For the next three days, we worked wrapped up in coats, scarves, and gloves. Teachers and students didn't find this unusual; they said this happened quite often. Teachers told us that the alarm system was unreliable, and from time to time the fire alarm drills required Galloway to run up and down the halls with a bell or just shout "Fire drill! Fire drill!"

Some twelve years later, in 1987, Galloway asked me to conduct a study of his school, a no-holds-barred study that would include a look at instruction, physical plant, finance, governance, student services, staff development, leadership, and anything else that could be brought under the microscope. The study took twelve months. Parents, students, alumni, faculty, community members, administration (which was mostly Elliott Galloway), and past and current board members all participated in the effort. The final product was a compendium of issues, anticipated issues, and a full set of recommendations complete with suggested implementation strategies. Galloway and the board of trustees signed off on the study. Shortly thereafter, he and the chair of the board invited me to lunch. Galloway then presented the challenge: since I knew the school so well and knew what needed to be done, it was really my professional responsibility to implement the recommendations. The only way it could be done was for me to agree to take over as head of the school.

I believed the study was sound, the recommendations were appropriate, I liked the school, and it was small. But was I, a five-year member of AARP, prepared to work that hard? After many discussions with my wife and some trusted colleagues, I decide to accept the challenge.

I had enjoyed much of my work at the university, even though I never believed we had made much difference in the lives of school leaders. The department of educational administration had allowed us to set up a principals' center, but the department never fully embraced the idea, nor did they accept the suggestion that practitioners needed to be much more involved in preparing school leaders. To some extent, that made the move a bit easier.

So this is how I ended up on the Friday before Labor Day weekend in 1990, sitting in a building that had no electrical power and no good prospects of getting any before school was to open on the following Tuesday. As it turned out, one of our board members knew a local contractor who was able to secure a new transformer, and an electrician who agreed to do the work.

In order to get a head start with the students, I decided to assist the girls softball coach; in the process I would meet many of the upper-school female students. It was a good decision. I was introduced to a nice cross section of young women of the nineties. They were outspoken and much bolder than I expected. One of the first issues to come up had to do with proper protocol in addressing the new assistant coach (who also happened to be the head of the school). Upper-school students had a long tradition of calling their teachers by their first names. Not wanting to appear indecisive, I suggested the Mr. Richardson would be appropriate. Fortunately, Elliott Galloway had set the tradition of "Mr.," so my decision didn't foment a rebellion.

The coach assigned me to the task of coaching first base. Prior to our first game and after giving me the full set of base running signals, I assumed my position in the coaching box. When our team came to bat, the first player singled sharply to left field, rounded first base, and decided to stay on first. I went to her and patted her on the back; immediately, the base umpire threw up his arms and declared the base runner was out. It seemed that the rule I had violated was that a coach may not touch a base runner. In fact his words were, "You have to keep your hands off the girls!" No doubt a reasonable request, but one that could have been conveyed to me in a more subtle fashion.

School seemed to get off to a fairly good start. Schedules were reasonably well arranged, and almost everyone was attempting to start off on the right foot. After a few mornings of observing car pool, I believed that it too was under control—that is, until about two weeks after school was under way, when a driver left his car unattended in the car pool line while he entered the school to make an emergency phone call. I stood frozen in place while the car pool process came to a complete standstill. Fortunately, one of the teachers had the presence of mind to get in and drive the car to a parking spot so traffic was able to move ahead. As the teacher got out of the car, she glanced at me with a look that seemed to say, "If you can't figure out what to do in a situation that seems to be such a no-brainer, what are you going to do when you face some real issues?"

Each day took on a life of its own. Everyone had to see me for some reason or another. The question "Could I see you for a minute?" took on a whole new meaning; the minute usually became about forty. (The other phrase I heard with increasing frequency in my first few years was "The Galloway Way." More about this a bit later.) In a small school, face-to-face communication takes precedence. To close the office door meant that the issue under consideration must be a matter of life and death. There was no place to hide. You were engaged from the moment you walked into the building until the moment you left; even then, you were accessible, because having an unlisted phone number was unheard of. Many issues were settled during conversations in the hallway; some issues took more time. I spent the better part of one morning with a group of six-year-olds attempting to explain why I had painted the outside of their art room and, in doing so, covered some of their artistic creations. I thought my explanation of color continuity and other such logical points would win the day, but they were not convinced that my decision had any credibility whatsoever.

Over the course of the next five years, we struggled with the many contradictions that seemed to be a part of this unique little school community. The interscholastic sports program was a good case in point. I had forgotten the emotion that was generated by high school interscholastic sports. It was even more interesting at the Galloway School, one with a distinguished history of being marked up on our competitors' schedules as "a game we will definitely win." The dilemma the school faced was that although we wanted everyone who was interested to be able to participate, there were some members of our community who felt that we should be competitive as well. The school supported a no-cut policy. This, taken literally, meant that any student interested in participating in our sports program could do so without fear of being cut from the squad. The only requirement was that as a participant, you had to follow one of the few rules the school did maintain: "Work hard and behave yourself."

There were some real problems here. First of all, the parents believed that we meant it. They interpreted the qualifier to mean that if a youngster attended all the practices and worked hard and behaved, then participation in games would be a logical next step. It seemed that our coaches believed that good behavior, hard work, and regular attendance at practice were important; but they also believed that a major objective was to win. There was absolutely no ambivalence about the importance of winning as far as our competitors were concerned. Our own community struggled with this problem. Our sports teams endured one defeat after another, and we were very aware of the embarrassment and confusion our athletes experienced as a result of the school's fuzzy view of competition. As a community, we agreed to face this issue and find a solution that was best for our students. At least we gave lip service to the well-being of our students; we hoped to find a way that would permit, indeed encourage, our students to be competitive while maintaining a balance and perspective that was healthy.

I think we all knew the problem would not be with the students; it would be with the adults. We began to try to find ways to arrive at a balance; we would never be a school known for its consistent winning record, but we did believe that it would be possible to create a competitive sports environment where the lessons of positive competitive involvement would be a recognized part of our educational program. Our solution was to retain the no-cut policy and create more teams, so that a youngster who wasn't talented enough to play at the varsity level would still have an opportunity to play competitively. But to some parents and students, this wasn't the Galloway Way. I thought this was a good time to go to the source, Elliott Galloway himself, and find out exactly what was meant by the Galloway Way.

Galloway entertained the question and responded with a question of his own. He asked me what I thought the phrase meant. I replied that it seemed to mean whatever the person using it wanted it to mean. His response was, "That sounds about right." Somewhat puzzled but not to be put off, I asked him how it was that as a very competitive athlete in his youth, who at age seventy was still running marathons, he had never been able to develop much of a competitive sports program. He pointed out that although there were very few successful teams with winning records, there were many successful individuals. Something to think about.

The issues faced in our sports program were illustrative of other issues we faced. How do you celebrate successes and good performance without doing it at the expense of others? How do you recognize faculty performance worthy of recognition without creating ill feelings or having it erode faculty morale? We wrestled with these issues; they were real and didn't lend themselves to nice, neat solutions. The more we explored ways to solve the various dilemmas, the more we heard the familiar refrain, "That is not the Galloway Way." If a student was confronted with not meeting an assignment deadline and a teacher proceeded to take action, the student would counter, "That isn't the Galloway Way!" If a faculty member wanted to try a new instructional approach, colleagues might respond, "That isn't the Galloway Way." A parental response to a decision to discipline a child for an inappropriate act might well use the same phrase.

However, the phrase wasn't used only as a means of rationalizing inappropriate behavior; it was also used in a positive fashion. For example, an act of disrespect, an attempt to take advantage of someone's weakness, rigid adherence to a rule or guideline that clearly indicated the absence of good common sense could also result in "That isn't the Galloway Way." It seemed to be both a deterrent and an enabler. There was no written set of rules that guided one to an appropriate use of the phrase. It was a starting point for a conversation. The guiding principles involved decency, respect, and common sense. The reason it was useful is because the school was small and people were accustomed to talking to each other.

Recently, a local newspaper reported an incident involving a middle school student who gave his French teacher a bottle of wine as a Christmas present. Because the school district had a zero-tolerance policy on alcohol, the student was suspended from school for ten days. As expected, the media made very good use of the event, and as a result there was a flood of letters to the editor, many of them heaping scorn on the school officials for such blatant lack of common sense.

There may have been more reasonable ways to handle this situation, but the school officials weren't the villains. There were no villains; the school was too large, and because of its size there were many rules and regulations that were rigorously administered. With more people, there are bound to be more rules and less opportunity to accommodate individual cases. Had this event taken place in a small school, chances are very good that a dialogue would have been initiated and a decision would have been made that was based upon common sense.

The Galloway School is a private school; the reason it works well has very little to do with the fact that it is private. It is a good school because the founder is a person of good will, who possesses a deep and abiding faith that all children can learn. He had the wisdom to create a small school. Any school that is organized around those principles, be it public or private, stands a good chance of being an effective school.

I have been away from the school for nearly three years. It remains a small school. There are a couple of new buildings. The electrical power plant's transformer is now eight years old and continues to function effectively. The organization of the car pool has been dramatically improved. The interscholastic sports program continues to baffle the community. Elliott Galloway, now in his late seventies, continues to run marathons. Rumor has it that any requests for painting the primary division facilities must be approved by the students. And the response to the latest attempt to allow the school to add one hundred more students was, "That is not the Galloway Way!"

JOE A. RICHARDSON *is a former public school teacher and administrator; he served as professor of educational administration, associate dean of the College of Education, and founder of the Principals' Center at Georgia State University. He has also served as headmaster of the Galloway School and is currently serving as a visiting practitioner at the Harvard Graduate School of Education.*

The term community of learners *is currently just about as common and revered as motherhood and apple pie. Bringing the concept to reality is far more difficult than baking an apple pie, however—though the need for ongoing nurturance and the degree of challenge are perhaps comparable to motherhood. This is the story of a practitioner who has lived with the struggles of trying to bring what she has learned about a community of learners from the International Network of Principals' Centers to the schoolhouse.*

8

Learning in the schoolhouse

Rebecca van der Bogert

I CONFESS: experiences in the Network have not always generated comfort within me. I've personally found our community of learners both a gift and a source of challenge. The gift is being with a group of people and experiencing something that is rare: total acceptance of the exploration of my new ideas, freedom to risk, support in trying out new things, and moments that feed my soul well beyond our being together.

So where's the challenge? Let me tell you a little bit about myself and you'll understand the source of dissonance. My heart is in public schools and I'm one of those people who can't leave well enough alone. When I'm involved in a unique experience or one of great meaning, I want to share it with others. Two such powerful experiences continue to stand out for me and remain a part of my being every time I walk down the hallway of a school. One, of course, is the experience you've heard about in the previous chapters of being

NEW DIRECTIONS FOR SCHOOL LEADERSHIP, NO. 7, SPRING 1998 © JOSSEY-BASS PUBLISHERS

part of a community of learners. The other is that of my graduate program.

Raised in a family that allowed nothing short of A's, and having attended a school that was clear about how one could earn them, I played the game well: listen to the teacher, do as you're told, and regurgitate the right information on tests. So imagine what I faced in a unique graduate program that asked thirteen of us as students to design our own courses and to grade ourselves. We had two professors to use as resources.

My first reaction to the program was one of immobility in response to the freedom. The second was emptiness, realizing I had no idea what I wanted to learn. The third was anger because I thought the professors weren't earning their money by producing a syllabus, telling me what to learn, and rewarding me with an A for doing what I'd been told. I slowly came to terms with the fact that the source of my anger was that *they* weren't filling my emptiness for me. I needed to.

The fourth stage was a painful and lengthy process of exploration and the emergence of "me" as a person and learner. I learned to face who I am, how I learn, what I believe in, what I want to learn, and above all what my own personal purpose is for learning. After many painful months, I emerged as a *passionate* learner committed to a lifetime of creating similar opportunities for others.

But that lifetime journey has not been easy. I left graduate school with the energy of an overexercised thoroughbred: ready to change the world and still free from any of the scars of life. One of my professors pulled me aside just before I left and with love and concern (and, I think, pity) urged me to find other believers along the way. I was perplexed by his comment until I later began to experience the same frustration I saw in my colleagues' faces about what was happening to children. It became even clearer when I was left with an overwhelming sense of powerlessness about not knowing where to turn to make things better. Like most of us, I found a close friend in my job with whom I could commiserate. Of course, we were considered the young rabble rousers. It wasn't until I began to meet various individuals in the Network that I felt I'd found not only a community of learners but a community of believers.

For three decades, my passion in schools has been fueled by a desire to bring to schools what I personally experienced in my graduate program as well as in the Network. From my graduate program, I bring a vision of a school that provides a rich environment for adults, filled with the opportunity to pursue their own passions, to learn that which is of importance to them and in the way that they learn best. From the Network, I bring a commitment to the power that comes from belonging to a community of learners, filled with the bond of a common mission, rich in conversations that evoke learning, surrounded by nurturing relationships that enhance learning, and permeated with a commitment to the greater sense of community.

My path has had ragged edges, partly because of a naïve approach to understanding how schools change, and partly because of the many entrenched practices we find in schools that counter the nurturing of growth experiences and at times seem intractable. But I have been blessed. Through the years, I have seen adults flourish as learners in schools, providing me with a yeasty opportunity to learn. And as an avid observer, I am clearer where the obstacles lie, and at times a little wiser about how to diminish them.

From answers to questions

As I look back through the years, my efforts have moved from trying to make changes to assisting others in defining their needs. Rather than thinking "the answer" for a school that nurtures adult growth is in a specific change such as a new method for staff development, I tend to look at a school as an organism and ask the bigger questions about the interaction of the various cells of the organism and the health of each cell.

I try to resist making generalities about schools. I've come to respect the uniqueness of each school, as I do individuals. What works for one school may not for another. I no longer enter a school with answers, but with questions. I've found it helpful in my understanding of schools to ask these questions in particular:

1. What is it that brings people together in this particular school?
2. What is the nature of relationships in this school, and how might we nurture those that enhance learning for adults?
3. Is there a commitment to the greater sense of community, and what might we do to nurture it?
4. Are there opportunities for the kind of conversation in schools that serves as a fruitful means of learning, and how might we expand on them?

With these four questions as a lens, I constantly challenge myself to identify specific elements I've experienced in the Network, to think about when I've seen them in schools, and to analyze what has caused or obstructed them.

Using the lens

First question: What is it that brings people together in schools?

If I reflect on our community of learners within the Network, it is clear that we have been brought together in a very different fashion from most school communities. We are not divided into committees, grade levels, or differentiated roles. We aren't sure from year to year when we will be meeting, who will show up, or who will run the meetings. We aren't always sure exactly what our tasks are, who is to do them, or what must get done. We aren't even sure who "we" are. If there's one thing that is predictable about our behavior, it's *flow*.

We are dead sure of some things, however. We are bonded together by a common passion: a need to understand and provide environments in which adult growth flourishes. We are also bonded by a common set of beliefs about teaching and learning and the importance of exploring how things happen around those beliefs. We know we can count on each other to give as much time and talent as we are able, and we understand when we can't. We believe we can make a difference together.

From time to time, I have seen these same elements in schools. It is rarely the result of a mandate from above or formation of a committee. It usually is a spontaneous gathering of a group of teachers who get excited about a concept and take the lead to explore its feasibility. They're there voluntarily, the rewards are intrinsic, and they are driven to make something happen that is of meaning to them.

I remember a librarian who became intrigued with the work of a particular artist. Before I, as principal, had any idea of what was happening, a large group of teachers were working together to bring his traveling exhibit to the school. The next thing I knew, the whole faculty organized an integrated day around his work. Every faculty member and student was involved in his work, with an excitement about their own learning and each other's learning that is rarely seen among students sitting in classroom rows or among teachers at a faculty meeting. You can imagine my surprise when the artist showed up!

It was clear to me that if as the principal I'd tried to organize such a project, it wouldn't have worked. It came from the teachers' interests, they organized themselves, and people joined voluntarily to be part of something greater than themselves and to have fun. I watched over the next couple of months to see if I could figure out what obstacles in the school prevented such a thing from ever happening again. It became clear that some faculty were used to pleasing authority; I had to free them from the shackles of the need to "cover" the curriculum and the idea that they had to ask permission to dream. I wanted to encourage the concept of exploring more deeply, rather than scurrying through the syllabus. This talk would have to be supported with resources and elimination of some current practices such as scheduling every minute with meetings, setting up committees, demanding reports, and so on. I also realized that an idea such as the one that seeded this project doesn't emerge in a pressured environment. Teachers require time to reflect, connect naturally, and discuss various ideas. They need incubation time. It wasn't something I could proactively make happen. My role was to avoid scheduling every minute of their time so that it *could* happen.

As I watched the spark of other teachers working together ignite and extinguish, I learned a great deal about the leader's role and my inadvertent ability to obstruct such activity. True, there were key moments when it was important that I know enough about the purpose for which people were coming together and the key players so that I could play the mediator of passions. But I didn't need to know so much that the demands of communication took away from teachers' time to work together. I also found it helpful if I could articulate for parents, and if necessary for the superintendent, the purpose and theory behind the project. In short, I found that I couldn't truly make anything happen. I had to clear the way so there would be time for ideas to emerge naturally, be available to assist in mediating through obstacles, provide resources, and articulate for the public what is gained.

As I attempt to do this, the obstacles become clear. One is the natural desire that educators have to take on too many ideas at once. Once the environment has provided time and permission for collaborating around ideas for a common purpose, it is such a natural force in people that a leader needs to moderate how much can be pursued at once—not *if*, but *when*. Another obstacle is fear of public opinion and the need to be accountable in the traditional sense (for example, through test scores, number of workshop hours, number of hours of time on task, and so on). This is where the leader's role of articulating the value of such collaborative projects comes into play, as well as the ability to ask the right questions so that the value for students is well thought out.

Second question: What is the nature of relationships that enhance adult learning, and how might we nurture them?

I've tried to make sense out of our own relationships in the Network to see if there is anything that could assist my work in the public schools. Among us, much remains implicit. It isn't said, but there is an assumption that we gather together to learn from one another, not through lecturing but through the conversations we have, through sharing our experiences and questioning, and through the projects we work on together. We have no titles or hierarchy. In fact, titles have been put on paper for the world to see us as an organization, but I'm not sure any of us know what our titles are. People are valued for what it is that they bring to the group and what it is that they might gain from the group. We know the art of asking for help and the art of giving help. We have come to know one another well enough over the years that there is a natural flow as to who meets different needs. If one of us wants to be comforted, we call Gayle; if one of us wants to be encouraged to continue the next chapter, we might call Gordy; to have our thinking stretched, Roland; to think through a difficult problem, Joe; and so on. We all know the other will be there if needed.

Naturally we all like each other, and there is a genuine kindness, but the connection is greater than that. We are there for a purpose—in fact, quite an ambitious purpose. We trust one another and are comfortable showing our vulnerabilities and sharing our mistakes. Competition rarely shows, and poking fun at oneself is common. In David's words, "We have connections that stay with us and support us even at a distance."

I've seen relationships such as these in schools from time to time. One of the most poignant examples of adult learning in a school district that I can remember took place among a group of teachers and administrators who joined together monthly with a consultant to look at the research question, What obstacles exist in the district that obstruct thinking both among students and adults? Participants volunteered to be a part of the project; release time was set aside; and rigorous analysis took place that involved reading, research, discussion, looking at oneself, and developing ways in which they might together make things happen within the district. There was true commitment on everyone's part because it was of prime interest to them intellectually as well as having direct impact on their professional lives. Many members of the group pursued graduate degrees on the topic, published articles about their work on the subject, and are now lecturing nationally.

When I do see an opportunity such as this, I try to determine what contributes, and what obstructs, events such as this from happening more often. One element that stands out is longevity. In the Network and in schools where I see these special relationships, it is usual that people have been together over time. In Gayle's words, "Memories have been built, filled with both humor and sadness." People know each other well enough that there is an implicit flow around each other's strengths and skills. Everyone knows specifically who to turn to for different needs. Because of this long-term commitment, there is the motivation to work through difficult issues; therefore the skills to do so have been developed. This presents many questions about how we might enhance longevity in school districts, particularly at the leadership level.

Another key element appears to be genuine support and sharing of one's learning rather than hiding it or any quality of competitiveness. I used to walk through the halls and ask myself what I saw that obstructed such relationships. The answer was all too obvious. Teachers spend the majority of their day in their own rooms. When they are together, much of the conversation is about logistics, such as recess duty, trading reading books, finding materials, and so on. Rarely do I or other teachers ask a teacher what she is passionate about or what he wants to learn. I also am cognizant of the many ways in which I as a leader inadvertently create distances among the adults in the building. I found this so in the formal evaluation process that I was expected to complete as a principal. No matter how close my relationship was with teachers, when it came time for a formal written evaluation the inadvertent message was, "I have the pen and am writing your evaluation; therefore I know what you should learn and how. I will also check in with you to see that you have learned it." We know what that does to the learner. Why do we continue to do it to teachers?

I also find that most discussion of test results inadvertently instills competition among teachers. How can teachers avoid inferring that they are judged by how well their test scores stack up, if the newspapers are comparing school against school? If it's a good measurement for school comparison, why not for teacher comparison?

Third question: What is the source of commitment to the greater sense of community, and what might we do to nurture it?

All of us have experienced the feeling of working with a group of people and forgetting oneself completely. There is no greater feeling. Some have gotten it on a basketball team, some in a pantry kitchen, others trimming a Christmas tree. When it happens in a school or a school district, it is magical!

Gayle describes it beautifully when she discusses relationships: "When we gather together, the common purpose and reason for being permeates all of what we do. There are celebrations of books published, discussions of who we are and where we want to be, and recognition is given and celebrated for contributing to the greater mission."

I've been fortunate to watch this happen in schools from time to time and am blessed currently to be a part of an administrative team that exhibits this sense every day. The expression "hands across the district" is used often, such as when particularly low test scores are received in one school, or when a group of parents are organizing to object to a multiage classroom, or just to deal with simple questions about what to do next.

When I do see this in schools, certain common elements seem to be present that also exist in our Network. The first is that members of the community are clear about the common purpose that is greater than the one held by each of them as individuals. Schools and school districts with a clear identity give members a good sense of why it is important to belong to the larger whole. These are usually districts that have provided time to question what it is they believe in and have crafted a document for all to see.

There also appears to be pride in being part of the whole as well, as a sense of history and culture. Very often schools that have this sense of community tell you that the school has had a sense of community for years. They often quote the history of the district or the building. I've actually seen archives set up in buildings, partly for their students' portfolios but also to exhibit documents about the schools. I've seen framed annual pictures of the whole staff on the front steps, events that incorporate the whole district, and storytellers who share the culture and pass it down to the next generation as part of new-teacher orientation. They know their roots.

There is usually recognition from colleagues about what each person gives to the whole—not to one another, but to the whole. There is also a quality that we're reticent to talk about in schools: spirituality. I have attended faculty meetings that better resemble Quaker meetings, or retreats with the most intimate of sharing and supporting.

I often see connected with all of this a teachers' association that assists in teachers' professional growth and understands the importance of resolving issues without creating divisiveness among roles or individuals.

Paradoxically, teachers tell you that they are committed to the school because of the autonomy that they are given; it seals their commitment to the whole.

The obstacles to such a sense of commitment are clear. One of them, I have concluded, is lack of longevity. Where you see this commitment, the average stay of an administrator or teacher far exceeds that in other places. This necessitates commitment to working through conflict in an open way that promotes growth. People get to know one another's strengths as well as weaknesses. They come to love and respect all aspects of one another as they live through many births and deaths together. They live a significant part of their lives together.

Along with this turnover of leadership comes confusion about direction and the foundation of beliefs. If teachers are asked to start a new initiative every two years when they know that it takes three to five years for anything to become part of a school culture, the transition leaves a school in a constant state of flux, responding to immediate and specific changes rather than asking questions about practice in regard to a solid set of beliefs.

Another element I observe in schools that have commitment to the greater sense of community is democratic involvement among those affected by decisions. Its absence is, of course, a major obstacle. Teachers feel part of a community if they know how decisions are made, if they're involved, and if the decisions are in sync with their beliefs about what should happen for children.

Fourth question: What forums for conversation exist in schools, and are they fruitful vehicles of learning?

I turn to Richard when I wonder about the nature of conversations that would enhance learning in schools. In his article, he describes so well the ones we have in the Network. Can we have conversations in schools that "honor all learners, celebrate their questions, support their quest for insight, nurture insights into action?" Can we gather such that "all members bring value to the circle" with an unpredictable "honesty and authenticity in language and form and structure?" Can each member of the conversation "suspend attachment to a particular point of view so the group can unfold deeper levels of attention, synthesis, and feeling?"

I've seen such conversations take place in schools. One example was when a principal made a concerted effort to provide an environment for just such conversations. He put aside some of the ongoing curriculum review and designated time to have discussions about what the staff believed in for children. He made the gatherings voluntary, and once the conversations were started, he let it flow. Follow-up sessions were planned and facilitated by the teachers. There was no role differentiation. I've also seen it happen when teachers gather in study groups around a topic of passionate interest and shared readings. It happens at faculty meetings when the business items are forgotten and a common concern is discussed.

But there are many obstacles to this kind of conversation happening. Time is always considered the enemy of educators. How can we have a philosophical discussion when teachers are anxious about phone calls to be returned, projects to be reviewed, newsletters to be written, and so on? The workload of teachers has changed tremendously as the public's expectations have changed. Communication is the key, but it takes more time.

Another obstacle is sheer numbers. In a time of fiscal constraint, numbers are increasing. There are more students per classroom, more faculty per building, and more building per district. This

runs counter to all of the research that supports smallness; smallness would in turn promote conversation.

The learnings

From graduate school to Network to my work in schools, I have
come to identify my biggest and toughest learnings.

From superhero to ethnographer

Perhaps my greatest learning curve was in the beginning, as I blun-
dered through with the arrogance of youth, convinced that I knew
exactly what schools should be like and acting as the benevolent
dictator who would provide the "right" environment for everyone
to learn. I so much wanted everyone to experience within their own
schools the joys and excitement that I had in graduate school. Fortunately, people were patient with me, and I eventually saw that I
could both learn and contribute a great deal by watching, listening,
and reflecting on my own behavior rather than acting as the hero
who was to make it happen for others. I've learned—the hard
way—the power of listening to others' reflections.

The power of modeling

I've also come to understand the powerful connection between creating a rich environment for adults in a school and student learning. As I join others in conversation about how we might enhance
adult growth, we struggle with many questions about our own
beliefs about teaching and learning. Inevitably these discussions
move to thoughtful reflection about the nature of classrooms. As I
see adults come alive to their own interests and learning, I see its
impact on students. What better motivator for a student than to
have an adult who is pursuing her own quest for knowledge?

From short-term solutions to a holistic view

The organic nature of schools presents itself to me repeatedly. As
we focus on various elements of the school that need to be modi-

fied to enrich the environment for adults, we find a mirror reflecting the interconnectedness of everything in a school and the degree to which we must attend to each piece. The modifications we make in one aspect of a school—for example, the evaluation instrument—has to be studied in regard to all other areas. I have come to respect the sensitivity with which one must address the impact that any move in a school has on all other facets of the school.

The fuel

These learnings have not come easily. They have come from making mistakes, feeling bruised, and often questioning if I could continue. But this questioning is only momentary, until my next conversation or meeting with someone in the Network. In the presence of a member of our community of learners, I am reminded of my passionate commitment to schools, my own excitement about learning, and the support that I have behind me. In the words of my professor of more than thirty years ago, "I have found myself a community of believers."

REBECCA (BECKY) VAN DER BOGERT *is the superintendent of schools in Winnetka, Illinois, and the codirector of the International Network of Principals' Centers at the Harvard Graduate School of Education.*

Roland Barth is always a step ahead of us. Just when we think we've figured out something in the present, he is contemplating the future and asking the difficult questions. Always done with a playful creativity that brings us together, he activates thoughtfulness in all of us.

9

From Puddle Dock to the twenty-first century

Roland S. Barth

As MY ODOMETER prepares to make the big revolution from 1999 to 2000, I find myself looking both back and ahead. Those of us whose careers have been dedicated to the development of school leaders are beginning to ask such questions as: What will schools of the twenty-first century be like? What would we *like* schools of the twenty-first century to be like? What would we like leadership for these schools to become? How might we make it likely that our attempts to generate leaders for schools of the future will yield fruit?

Sometimes, the best way to look forward is to first look backward.

In the 1940s, along with a couple of dozen other rural scholars, I attended the one-room schoolhouse at Puddle Dock in Alna, Maine. I remember well portions of this experience; others have happily been forgotten, perhaps repressed.

After packing up our lunch buckets, my brother, my sister, and I marched without enthusiasm the half mile to the end of Nelson Road. The diminutive yellow school bus arrived, unfortunately on

NEW DIRECTIONS FOR SCHOOL LEADERSHIP, NO. 7, SPRING 1998 © JOSSEY-BASS PUBLISHERS

schedule. At the wheel sat Bill Humason, a soft-spoken gentleman with a twinkle in his eye, who lived and maintained a wonderful little farm in Alna Center.

About amidships on the same vehicle resided the ominous hulk of Suzy Humason, Bill's wife. It was her duty—her pleasure—to ensure complete silence on the bus, a duty she fulfilled with distinction and intimidation. There was fire, not twinkle, in Suzy's eye. I remember concluding what I thought was a carefully concealed conversation with my assigned seatmate, only to be severely cuffed about the head and shoulders by a blunt instrument: Suzie's fist. The follow-up punch was a withering glare.

Once at school, the boys entered through the right-hand door, the girls by the left. (As a boy, it was good sport to see if you could use the wrong portal and get away with it.) Once inside, we were warmed by the potbellied stove at the front of the room. This did a better job of keeping the nearby teacher and students warm than it did the others. Perhaps this is why some of us misbehaved so frequently: so we would be reseated forward. The teacher's cold glower was small price to pay for the stove's warm glow.

The scholars were cooled by a bucket of spring water at the back corner, from which we drank with a common dipper, one at a time—with permission, of course, the request signaled by one hand raised. Occasionally a foreign object found its way into the bucket, a huge frog for instance, strikingly similar to the one I had seen on the way to school.

Beside the bucket were two doors leading to separate portions of the same outhouse. Permission was usually gained if two hands were waved with sufficient urgency. Inside the privy, privacy between the boys' and the girls' portions was assured by a partition whose knotholes were occasionally breached by naughty boys. This sport prevailed only when the teacher lost track of how many students she had given permission to use these facilities.

Lessons began with the youngest students, who sat in a row at the left. Once the teacher had completed perhaps ten minutes of reading instruction with the six-year-olds, she moved to the next row, then the next, and so on, until mercifully she reached the oldest youngster at the right side. (I don't know if *she* felt relieved, but I know I did!) Whereupon, back to the left she went for another sweep in handwriting, then another in. . . .

Those of us who found listening to these incessant lessons tedious, boring, or impossible managed to indicate this in a variety of covert or occasionally quite overt ways. Whenever we injected into our diction some barroom swears, out came the bar of Lava soap. I remember being commanded to hold my unruly friend while his mouth was cleansed by the diminutive teacher, whereupon it became his turn to restrain me as I received my oral hygiene. The lingering taste of this treatment usually served to keep our insults to the teacher, or to one another, in check for a day or two.

After the effectiveness of the soap washed away, an array of switches and sticks waited behind the door in the boys' (for some reason, only the boys') entry way. There was some democracy, however; the teacher allowed us to select which it would be: a willow switch or a stout oak stick. We usually preferred the dull stick, which in the hands of the weak teacher did less damage than the sting of the sharp switch. On one occasion, the teacher went to the arsenal and was chagrined to discover that all of the sticks and switches had inexplicably disappeared.

Recesses were all too infrequent and all too brief. We were confined to a simple swing set at which the boys and girls bantered and teased. There was quite a bit of loose gravel about; this afforded good ammunition, because only when we actually succeeded in *hitting* the bell atop the school was recess a true success. The teacher promptly stormed out of the building looking for (and never finding) the perpetrator of the lovely, sought-after tone. That was the best of all recess games.

Lunch was taken in the schoolyard, rain or shine. We were allowed perhaps a precious fifteen minutes to take inventory of one another's dinner boxes, effect our exchanges of peanut butter for tuna fish, and belt them down. Thence back to arithmetic and another sweep across the room.

Finally, at precisely three o'clock, the teacher (this time) rang the schoolhouse bell. The girls were allowed a safe exit first, before the boys exploded out of the confining container but immediately onto another confining container, superintended by Ms. Humason. As each of us exited the bus, appropriate hand signals were the customary punctuation with which to end the school day.

Somehow we all emerged from the tortured minutes and days of fear, boredom, and routine sufficiently educated to be promoted to another year of the same. Ah yes, that which does not destroy us makes us stronger. My mother assured me that each day and each year I endured at the Puddle Dock school was "character building." I agree with her. Yet to this day, I'm not sure just what the character was that it built.

The real learnings

My years of servitude at the Puddle Dock School provided a solid reference point. During my subsequent career on the other side of the desk, as teacher, principal, and professor, I have mused at the complaints of today's students about the cafeteria food, about the "mean" teacher, about the problems on the bus, about the workload, and about the too-cold classroom.

I learned a great deal during my years attending the one-room schoolhouse. The experience continues to generate new learnings:

- Smallness does not inevitably bring with it a culture of intimacy and hospitality for learning.
- A sense of community can persist even in the face of fear and oppression.
- Leadership in small schools is direct, visible, and palpable—for better or for worse.
- Communities of learning take many forms.

And I learned that I, for one, have no wish to return to the good old days!

Looking forward

Today, I remind myself that life in the Puddle Dock School in the 1940s probably bears as much resemblance to schools of the 1990s as today's schools will have for those of the mid-twenty-first century. To be sure, all of these attempts to provide what we elegantly call "formal education" will continue to have much in common: a curriculum, teachers, learners, and places for learning. Yet other characteristics will certainly differ: rewards and punishments, physical facilities, grouping of youngsters, what students are supposed to learn, the nature of that leaning, the role of the teacher, and the role of the school leader.

It's difficult—but fun—to predict what the schools of the next century will look like. Many, I'm afraid, seem en route to becoming a combination of a nineteenth-century factory in Lowell, a twentieth-century penal colony in Attica, and the twenty-first century Educational Testing Service in Princeton.

I prefer to go along with Peter Drucker, who has observed that "if you want to predict the future, create it." This is precisely what I have been about. For the past several months, I have been working with a team of remarkable educators in Providence, to envision schools for the twenty-first century as we would like to see them. Our task has been to design a program that selects educators and prepares them to become principals for those desirable schools of the future.

Dennis Littky and Elliot Washor are coprincipals of the Metropolitan Center (MET), a small, innovative, public secondary school in Providence. Formerly, they enjoyed together some turbulent years at Thayer High School in Winchester, New Hampshire. Jay Casbon, a former principal, is dean of the graduate school at Lewis and Clark College in Portland, Oregon. Lewis and Clark will provide the academic umbrella and principal certification for the new program. Finally there is Farrell Allen; she is the observer and scribe who heroically attempts to convert our oral conversations into the written word. "Flirtatious anarchists" all!

For several days, the five of us sequestered ourselves in the living room of Dennis's modest nineteenth-century tradesman's house near the Providence docks. We took turns at the rocker, the couch, and the straight-back chairs assembled around a little table. We munched candy bars, nachos, and drank cider and soda—all the while provoking one another to dream what we want our schools to be like in the next century. In some ways, decidedly unlike Puddle Dock School! Yet now that I think of it, it is in other respects very much like that one-room schoolhouse.

These conversations turned to inventing a series of experiences that we believe will generate capable leaders for schools of the twenty-first century. I would like here to draw upon our work, which is based largely upon a knowledge base of experience. We value and trust the educative powers of experience. We value and trust our own experiences and what we have learned from them about leadership and the preparation of leaders.

Collectively we have spent nearly two hundred years of residence in and around schools: as students in schools, parents of students in schools, teachers in schools, teachers of teachers, principals of schools, teachers of aspiring and practicing principals for schools, and consultants to schools. We believe these experiences entitle and equip us to dream and design a bit.

The richness of each other's experience has come as no surprise to us. What is surprising is the degree of congruence in what we have learned from our very different experiences. Thus all of what follows is to be prefaced with "on the basis of our experience, we believe. . . ." For me, this runs the gigantic gamut from the Puddle Dock School to the Harvard Graduate School of Education.

We first addressed the question, "What would we *like* schools of the future to be like?" and responded unanimously: "Small." Ours is the ongoing quest to create environments in which human learning and growth flourish. For us, this means from ten to four hundred students, and from one to thirty staff members. In such an environment, we believe it possible (although, as the one-room schoolhouse suggests, not inevitable) that an intimate, personal, democratic, student-centered learning environment can be created.

In a small school as we envision it (and as Littky and Washor now conduct it), a rich range of resources are available: books, computers, maps, science equipment, animals. But equally important is recognition of and full use of resources that reside *outside* the school: in the community libraries, museums, workplaces, woods, and streams. Of course, there are abundant personal resources, which include paid teachers and staff, volunteers, parents, visitors, and community members. As Dennis Littky says, "I want to use *everybody* as the teachers of students." In short, we believe that the world is the ultimate schoolhouse.

Given these resources, the purpose of school is to get students' learning curves (and those of the educators of students) off the chart, that is, to provide the conditions making it likely that everyone discovers the import, the excitement, frequently the difficulty, and the life-renewing force that accompanies being an insatiable learner. Along the way, one develops new skills of inquiry, which include posing one's own problem, assembling resources for addressing it, forming an hypothesis, sticking with the work persistently through thick and thin, learning, and periodically articulating that learning orally and in writing.

It is commonly believed that a school succeeds if all its students test above average—even if they subsequently burn their books and their bridges to future learning. We, on the contrary, believe a school succeeds only if, after graduation, students' learning curves *continue* off the chart.

It has been estimated that today's students graduate from high school knowing perhaps only 2 percent of what they need to know in order to be successful in the workplace, at home, and in life. Ninety-eight percent is yet to come. Without question, the most critical "graduation requirement," then—perhaps the *only* really important graduation requirement—is evidence that each student emerges from the school experience demanding not less but *more* learning and is capable of providing it independently. All schooling in the present must be about lifelong learning in the future.

We believe that these kinds of schools will be created if, and only if, there is a good leader. Our experiences suggest that behind every good school is a good leader. Good leadership for a small school is that which helps create and nourish this kind of learning environment. Leadership for small schools is caring, moral, reflective, visionary, risk-taking, modeling, learning, and shared.

The design principles

The exciting—and formidable—question we are confronting is, "How do you select and prepare good leaders for these small schools of the next millennium?" On the basis of our very different life experiences, a number of important "design principles" emerged through the haze of Dennis's pipe smoke. These principles now direct our work and characterize the new program.

Collaboration with an exemplar

We believe that the best, perhaps the only, way for an able, bright, motivated educator to become a distinguished principal is to work closely and continuously with a distinguished principal (and with the other school leaders who inevitably surround good principals) for a sustained period. In the case of the program suggested here, that would be for two years.

Apprenticeship is a concept that for several millennia has been recognized as the most obvious, most powerful means for those who don't know how, and want to learn how, to acquire the characteristics of the accomplished practitioner. The apprenticeship has been around far longer than has formal, academic coursework.

Only when an aspiring principal, within the crucible of the schoolhouse, takes on little by little the work of the accomplished mentor, under the continual guidance of the mentor, in constant association with the mentor, and with the enthusiastic support and commitment of the mentor, can we begin in any real sense to "prepare" a principal.

Walking the talk

Any experience deemed valuable and essential for students, we believe, is valuable and essential for aspiring and practicing principals. Portfolios, exhibitions, writing, teamwork, and community service are experiences essential to all lifelong learners.

The schoolhouse is the place

Schools and the communities that surround them can be powerful contexts for student and teacher development. The schoolhouse is also the most promising locus for the development of principals.

One set of books

The primary work of the educator is to promote human learning. Leadership skills are developed through continuous practice, reflection, and conversation, and by learning to make judicious use of educational research. Every bit as important is clarification and articulation of craft knowledge through practitioner-generated research.

These skills are seldom developed by working in school all day with children and then attending a class on child development at night. We believe the different knowledge bases about teaching, learning, leadership, and school improvement must be integrated in time and place. We believe it essential that the lives of aspiring school principals be characterized not by two disparate "sets of books" but by one coherent set of books. Learning takes place best in a context relevant to it.

Learning from experience is not inevitable

All school practitioners have experiences. Lots of them. Too few experiences are instructive and instrumental in helping improve practice and the practitioner. Promoting adult learning through experiences acquired within the schoolhouse requires deliberate, rigorous, imaginative organization and planning. Deriving insight and wisdom from experience and then subsequently modifying practice based on new learning demands intentionality. Above all, gleaning the nuggets from the gravel requires constant association with a distinguished principal who models the skills of the reflective practitioner.

The greater the diversity, the greater the learning

In schools, we tend to group our differences as best we can, as fast as they appear—difference of ability, social class, special needs, gender—in the name of promoting teacher performance and pupil achievement. Our experiences in schools suggest that it is *maximizing* rather than minimizing differences among a group of learners that is associated with the steepest learning curves.

The learner owns the learning

One can attempt to teach a student or an aspiring principal, but one cannot learn for him or her. We believe that each principal in preparation is ultimately responsible for designing, fostering, and assessing his or her own learning. It is the responsibility of the program to support this learning through a network of aspiring principals, mentors, conversations, collective summer experiences, careful advising, and the like. Rather, it is our intent to continuously take inventory and value what each aspiring principal already knows and can do and assist the principal in moving to what is beyond. That is to treat them like the grown-ups they are.

Leading and learning are personalized

We believe in small schools. The most powerful learning experiences we observe occur in intimate learning environments of tangible scale. We believe that it is impossible to create an effective learning community in a large school. "A learning community of three thousand" is oxymoronic. To develop effective leaders and effective schools requires personalized scale. It makes little sense for any of us working hard to provide distinguished preparation for principals and then place them in a setting that nullifies their abilities.

Value the present

It is common wisdom that students who constantly see the connection between what they are doing in school and the so-called real world are more motivated, learn more, and value their learning. If the activities of students prepare them for some distant, abstract world, their education has little meaning for them.

Similarly, aspiring principals who "play school"—read assignments, write papers, take exams—on the assumption that one day this will help them offer outstanding leadership to their schools will be disappointed both as students *and* as school leaders.

In this program of ours, school and the real world for aspiring principals are synonymous and indistinguishable. Although the purpose here is to prepare educators for the principalship, the program isn't only about preparation. The work must be real and useful, *now*.

The big picture

The primary mission of our program is to select and prepare leaders for small schools of the twenty-first century. We believe strongly that, in addition to becoming outstanding principals, educators also have a responsibility to be change agents who replenish the profession. The program provides experiences that link improvement of a public school with improvement of public education.

Value midcourse corrections

A great program, like a great leader, must have the ability to constantly read what is happening and to adapt quickly—in short, to invent on the spot. The best organizations are organic and self-correcting. Therefore, although we have a long-term dream, we do not have a long-term lesson plan for the program. We offer a careful two-year, short-term plan with the intent to take regular soundings and make changes in response to unexpected problems and opportunities. What we visualize today may not become the program of tomorrow. But the dream of tomorrow is more likely to be realized if we unburden ourselves from rigid plans for a distant, unpredictable future.

Foundational beliefs

We believe a program that acknowledges and takes seriously these design principles fosters both outstanding principals and outstanding schools.

Our experience suggests that inherent in these principles are the conditions most likely to promote the kind of learning in aspiring principals that equips them to become outstanding leaders of the growing number of small schools of the future.

The learning environment of students—whether fourth graders, high schoolers, teachers in training, or aspiring principals—is all too information-rich and experience-poor. I would estimate that about 80 percent of students' time in schools is spent taking in, attempting to memorize, and then sending back information. Learners are bombarded by, saturated with, and then expected to display on demand information about wars, the periodic table, algebraic algorithms, the parts of speech, and school law.

A transmission-of-knowledge model of learning seems to pervade formal education. For too long, it has driven our profession. This model (Figure 9.1) is based on several assumptions:

- A body of knowledge, K, exists, consisting of everything recorded from Plato to nuclear physics. If you want to see it, you can go to the Widener Library at Harvard.

- The purpose of education is to transmit as much of this K to students as fast as possible.

- Because there is too much K to convey to students, a selection is made from it (C, the curriculum), which is deemed most essential for students of a given age to "know."

- The curriculum is conveyed to an agent A, usually a teacher, but possibly a computer, a program, or film, whose job it is to transmit it to students.

- Whether in middle school or in a department of educational administration, students are evaluated on the basis of how much of

Figure 9.1. Transmission-of-knowledge model of learning

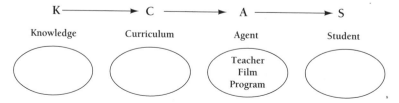

the *K* they acquire between September and June each year. These evaluations are thought to reveal how much each has learned.

I believe that those who participate in this model—teachers, students, administrators, parents—are engaged in playing school. They participate in an activity that appears respectable, rigorous, readily evaluated, and purposeful. The only problem with the model is that students don't learn very much from it. One estimate is that we remember in six weeks perhaps 5 percent of what has been transmitted to us in this way. Even knowledge transmitted through Suzie Humason's fist has dissipated with time!

Another problem with the transmission-of-knowledge model is that it creates on the part of students a culture of both resistance and dependency. If the teacher, the structure, and the grades are withdrawn, for all too many students learning ceases. I recently visited a high school just before graduation and observed students throwing away their books and notes and shouting, "Never again!"

It is our intention with the 21st Century Leadership Program to replace the venerable transmission-of-knowledge model and create for aspiring principals (who we expect will subsequently create for teachers and students in their schools) a very different, "experiential" model of learning (Figure 9.2).

As we have written elsewhere:

This principal preparation program allows aspiring principals to learn leadership in carefully selected small schools throughout the country and the world. The Internship consists of working in a school under the guidance of a distinguished, practicing principal and taking on increasing leadership responsibility in the school over a two-year period. Aspiring principals and

Figure 9.2. Experiential model of learning

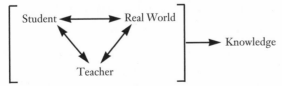

the exemplar principals from all of the program sites gather at summer institutes as well as networking throughout the two years to share resources and ideas. Through the 21st Century Leadership Program, aspirants master the craft of small-school leadership and learn through Lewis and Clark College certification as public schools principals.[1]

Each student, be she a fourth grader or an aspiring principal, places herself or is placed in association with a piece of the "real world" (*RW* in Figure 9.2). For a primary school student, this might be association with a battery, bulb, and wire on his desk; for the principal in preparation it might be a committee of the PTA or the building of a playground. Whereas in most schools the teacher determines the question for students to pursue, in this model the questions emerge from the interaction of student with the real world. The students themselves pose questions, which are evoked for them and with which they are occupied: "How can I light the bulb?" This is the meaning of "ownership" of one's own learning.

A teacher (or in the case of the program, the mentor principal), *T*, is instrumental in helping select and provide the piece of the real world with which the student is occupied. The teacher also offers support, challenge, counseling, a role model, and periodic opportunities to debrief the experience. In short, the teacher helps the student extract, analyze, clarify, and articulate her learning from experience.

From this interaction between student, teacher, and the real world, some knowledge emerges. The nature of this knowledge (in contrast to the transmission-of-knowledge model) is personal and idiosyncratic. One student may have learned how to light the bulb, another how many batteries were needed to burn it out! One aspiring principal may have learned some new skills in leading a group, another how to differentiate a friendly parent from an unfriendly one.

My colleagues and I in this endeavor believe that the experiential model of learning holds powerful potential for transforming the nature and amount of learning that can occur in the educational setting called *school*. We would like to see it occupy perhaps 80 percent of a student's day or program, rather than 20 percent.

This model may not look or sound like school; it may not always connote legitimacy, rigor, and hard work. But it has stood each of us in good stead in our own educations and in our work with others. When we ask successful school leaders, "How did you learn to provide good leadership?" most respond, "From experience," or from observing a great school leader, or on the job. Few report acquiring these skills through formal coursework at universities.

Furthermore, the experiential model offers training in independence. After living in an environment that is experience-rich and learning-filled, students leave "school" able to encounter new situations with confidence, learn from them, and retain far more than 5 percent of that learning. In short, they become lifelong learners. We observe daily the astonishing results of the experiential model at the MET. Beginning in June 1998, we expect to observe more such results in the program to prepare leaders for schools of the twenty-first century.

We want nothing less than to see a cadre of new school leaders entering our profession who are lifelong learners themselves, modeling the most important purpose of a school; leaders who value and trust learning from experience for themselves and who know how to rigorously craft and structure experience so that it yields important personal learning for students, teachers, and parents. We want to see school principals willing to take the big risks necessary to ring the bell atop the schoolhouse of the twenty-first century, so that it may become both a community of learners and a community of leaders.

Note

1. Barth, R., Casbon, J., Littky, D., and Washor, E. "Generating Leaders for Schools of the Twenty-First Century." Providence, R.I.: Big Picture Co., 1998.

ROLAND S. BARTH *is a former public school teacher and principal, founding director of the Harvard Principals' Center, and senior lecturer on education at the Harvard Graduate School of Education. He writes and sails in Florida and Maine.*

Index